Herbs and Spices

Herbs and Spices

Linda Gray

Skyhorse Publishing

Skyhorse Publishing books may be purchased in bulk at special discounts for sales promotion, corporate gifts, fund-raising, or educational purposes. Special editions can also be created to specifications. For details, contact the Special Sales Department, Skyhorse Publishing, 307 West 36th Street, 11th Floor, New York, NY 10018 or info@skyhorsepublishing.com.

Skyhorse® and Skyhorse Publishing® are registered trademarks of Skyhorse Publishing, Inc.®, a Delaware corporation.

www.skyhorsepublishing.com

10 9 8 7 6 5 4 3 2

ISBN 978-1-61608-523-0

Library of Congress Cataloging-in-Publication Data is on file.

Printed in China

Disclaimer:

The author and publishers have made every effort to ensure that all information given in this book is safe and accurate, but they cannot accept liability for any resulting injury or loss or damage to either property or person, whether direct or consequential or however arising.

CONTENTS

INTRODUCTION

Over the past couple of decades or so, processed sugars and excess salt have infiltrated our diets and changed the way we perceive pleasurable tastes. The increased focus on healthy eating and the vogue for growing your own food has helped promote the idea of exploring new tastes, and steering the family's taste buds away from sugary snacks to appreciating good food and natural flavours.

Herbs and spices that you grow yourself can do just that, and even if you have never grown a plant before, herbs are a good place to start, whether you have a large garden or just an available windowsill.

The difference between herbs and spices is simply the part of the plant used. The leaves and flowers of plants are generally regarded as the herbs while the seeds, roots, stigmas, and even bark are considered to be spices.

For many thousands of years, herbs been considered as magical plants—humans have used them for millennia as food and as medicine. Those who knew what to do with herbs were sometimes treated with suspicion and sometimes revered. Spices, on the other hand, were shrouded in mystery until recent times—their exotic nature and origins were mythologized by the spice traders over the centuries to keep the prices as high as possible.

In our present information-packed world we can have it all, and growing herbs and spices at home is one of the most satisfying projects anyone can take on. The wonderful tastes of herbs and spices can encourage even the most jaded palate to enjoy good food again. And the more good food we eat the less we want the stuff that is not so good for us.

Planning a herb garden

There is a lot to be said for letting your garden grow wild to provide a mini-ecosystem for bees, butterflies, and wildflowers; however, if you actually want to produce crops for you and your family to eat, it's necessary to do a little planning.

How to begin

Herbs and spices can be grown in different places around the garden; for example, it's always a good idea to have a basil plant growing with your tomatoes every year, but many herbs are perennial and will benefit from having their own space. A custom-made herb garden can thrive for years with very little maintenance, given the right conditions and a little TLC from time to time. One of the best ways to maintain herbs is to actually pick them and use them; it is easy to overlook small herbs but most will benefit if used regularly.

Herbs and spices are very accommodating plants and most will be happy in containers, so if you are short of outdoor garden space, growing in pots is an ideal alternative.

As with any sort of gardening, it's best to first decide what you want to grow and then do a little research to make sure it's feasible in your part of the world—growing mangos outdoors in a cool temperate climate is probably a non-starter.

What to grow

The first step to planning your herb garden is to decide what to grow. Firstly, choose those herbs and spices your family likes to eat. The second consideration is your particular climate and soil and then the space you have available for this kind of project. The herbs and spices listed in this book are for culinary use, although most have other uses in preventative medicines and cures for minor ailments.

If you use a lot of tomatoes in the kitchen, then basil is a must in your herb garden since it enhances the flavor of tomatoes, especially home-grown ones. Basil is an annual herb in moderate climates and needs to be sown every year, but other herbs such as thyme, sage, and mint will come up on their own year after year. Aloe vera is a useful herb, especially in the kitchen as the sap from the leaves can be used to soothe minor burns; it is grown commercially now for its healing properties and is added to many products. Read through the descriptions and growing requirements of the herbs and spices in this book and note down the ones that appeal to you and that you think you might like to grow. A little planning goes a long way here, but don't get bogged down in too much detail.

Where to grow

Deciding where to grow your herbs and spices is the next most important step after choosing your seeds or plants. You will probably have some idea already from when you researched which herbs to grow—some need to be grown indoors or in a greenhouse while others may prefer full sun or partial shade. Always take into consideration the preferred environment for each plant. Many plants will run to seed in hot midday sun but many need some sun during the day.

Preparing the space

Although it is not essential in most cases, you might check the pH balance of your soil since some plants won't tolerate very acidic soil. Get the balance right and you will produce better crops.

Avoid digging over a large patch as soon as the weather allows it. Unless you do a physical day job, the chances are that prolonged digging of heavy soil will result in an aching back and could put you out of garden action for weeks. It can also discourage you from continuing. Take it slowly if you are preparing a large plot—a little digging every day will get the job done and it won't feel so much like a chore.

Some people are put off the idea of gardening because they have the impression that gardening is back-breaking work, but this doesn't have to be the case. If you are physically challenged or aren't inclined to get stuck into the digging, employ someone else to do the job for you, which will mean that you have all of the pleasures and not too much hard work!

Remove any perennial weeds, large stones and non-organic debris from the soil and hoe or rake the soil to a fine consistency before planting young plants or sowing seeds.

Designing a herb garden

Space permitting, a specially designed herb garden is a delightful addition to any garden. It doesn't have to be large—herbs are very accommodating and many will be happy to grow closely together in a small space. Herbs can be grown along the borders of a flowerbed, in a raised bed, or you could adopt the French *potager* design idea where vegetables are grown in small beds with herbs fringing all of the edges.

This is a good plan if you are growing other crops since the strong scents of herbs and spices help deter bugs and viruses from fruit and vegetable crops. Otherwise simply have a herb bed as small or large as your garden can cope with.

Containers

There are very few herbs that can't be grown in containers. You can find containers in all shapes and sizes and a good garden center will have a variety to suit your particular needs. If you are planning to grow plants in large containers or tubs, consider mobility. It may be worthwhile investing in a pot mover if the plants need to be moved indoors or into a greenhouse or conservatory during the winter months.

Containers should be moved around from time to time to prevent insects and other wildlife taking up residence in or under the pot. They should always be well drained, and preferably placed on a stand to allow for air circulation and drainage. Never let your containers dry out. With a few exceptions, water is essential for the full development of your plants.

Look out for old pots and containers in charity shops or car boot sales. A few antique-style pots artfully arranged on a patio planted up with thriving herbs can look spectacular. Plain pots can be painted or glazed and personalized to suit your outdoor décor or to enhance the color scheme in your kitchen.

Dealing with pests

Herbs and spices are naturally a gardener's friend, since many possess strong scents that deter a number of bugs, especially tiny but destructive aphids. Carefully position herbs around the garden, even if they are in containers, to shield your vegetables and other crops from pests. Luckily, bees are very attracted to the flowers of herb and spice plants, so if you have a plentiful supply of these, the bees will love your garden and help pollinate other crops.

One problem that never seems to go away is the slug and snail population. Given the chance, there are few young plants that slugs won't eat. Protect your young plants in whatever organic way possible—a bowl of beer is said to distract slugs from plants, and crushed eggshells spread around the plants' stems will stop these gastropods for a while. Dry sand spread in a similar way helps for a time but as soon as it gets wet, slugs take no notice of it at all.

Get the birds to help out; dig over a patch of ground and walk away, allowing the waiting birds to collect any unearthed slugs and snails. If you can do this at the crack of dawn when the birds are hungry, so much the better. The only downside is that encouraging the birds will also put your seeds at risk. Use wildlife-friendly netting and cover all lines of seeds and young seedlings for a few weeks until plants are growing well.

Pest Control

Grow a couple of garlic plants in the rose bed and always include a few in the vegetable garden to deter aphids.

A pot of basil growing on a windowsill will help prevent flies from entering the house.

Recycle, reuse, restore

A trip to the garden center can be expensive even if you are only stocking up on a few basic seed trays or pots. Before making an expensive trip, have a good look around your own home—lots of packaging and containers can be utilized in the garden, and you will be doing your bit for the environment as well as saving some cash.

Pots

Save yogurt and dessert-type plastic pots throughout the year for seed sowing and bringing on seedlings. Wash and dry thoroughly and store in a recycling box until they are needed. Punch holes in the bottom of each pot for drainage.

The inner cardboard tubes from kitchen and toilet paper rolls make perfect biodegradable pots. They may need cutting in half or trimming. Squash the tubes together in a tray when sowing seeds and they should last long enough to be planted straight out into the garden or repotted.

Trays

Recent decorating projects may have left you with a couple of paint trays hanging around. Wash and dry well, punch a few holes in the bottom for drainage and keep these in the recycle box. Ask your friends and neighbours if they have any spare paint trays they don't want.

Plastic covers

A mineral water bottle cut in half can be transformed into two mini-greenhouses and will protect individual plants from cold nights. Clear plastic sheeting from packaging should also be saved and can be turned into small makeshift cloches, which are invaluable in early spring.

Cutlery

Keep a couple of old spoons or forks from the cutlery drawer for the garden. They are ideal tools for dealing with small plants in a greenhouse or potting shed.

Look out for garden possibilities before you commit anything to the rubbish. Large clean tin cans and old metal buckets can be transformed into interesting planters once you've made some drainage holes in the bottom. Old chimney pots, wooden crates, and wine boxes all have garden use potential.

Get the kids involved

Save lollypop sticks, straws, and other paraphernalia for pot markers and seed rows. Getting the kids to collect stuff for a project now will help generate lots of interest in the garden later on.

One plant, several uses

Many plants produce edible herbs as well as spices so you are able to use the plant to its full capacity, and in some cases, plants can also be used as a vegetable, making them three times the value. The four plants within this chapter are extremely versatile: celery and fennel can be used as a vegetable, a spice, and a herb, while coriander and nasturtiums can be used as herb and spice and all are easy to grow in most climates.

Plant diversity

Nature provides us with all the nutrients and vitamins our bodies need to be healthy and sometimes plants we classify as common weeds are actually very worthy plants to grow and eat. Dandelion (*Taraxacum officinale*), for example, tends to grow as a weed in many habitats around the world and is difficult to get rid of in the vegetable garden. However, it is also a very practical plant, and can be used rather than dug up and thrown on the compost heap.

For example, the roots of dandelions can be roasted and used as a caffeine-free coffee substitute. Young dandelion leaves can be added to salads and if too bitter, the leaves can be blanched much like spinach before eating. The sap from the stem is reputedly an effective cure for warts and verrucas. And last but not least, the flowers can be made into a delicious and healthy jam and also into dandelion wine.

If the simple dandelion can provide us with so many useful "products," it's no surprise that many other plants do the same. In this chapter, we look at four plants found in the home garden that will give you at least two products for the price of one.

Celery

Although celery is generally eaten as a vegetable and a healthy low-calorie snack food, it is a herb. Cultivated for thousands of years, celery was considered an important plant in Roman times when it was used for its flavoring abilities and medicinal properties. Until the seventh century the leaves, seeds, and roots were all used; Italian gardeners during this time discovered that by blanching the stems (by earthing up, see page 20), a tasty vegetable could be produced. Celery seeds are crushed and used as celery salt, while the leaves can be used to flavor almost any dish.

Wild celery (*Apium graveolens*) is a biennial plant producing wide stems from a fleshy root during its first year of growth and then flowers and seeds the following year. Although wild celery can still be found growing wild in many parts of Europe, America and Africa, it won't produce the stems we eat as a vegetable unless the plant is blanched and cultivated specifically for the stems. Some hybrid varieties of celery may not over-winter in cooler climates but can be protected by a cloche or similar cover if seeds are required.

Growing advice

Although celery is a hardy biennial plant and will over-winter in many areas, it does need warmth for the seeds to germinate. Check your seed packet for the manufacturer's sowing and growing recommendations, but generally celery seeds can be started in early spring.

Sowing

Fill well-drained pots or trays with fresh compost and sow seed fairly sparingly. Celery seeds can take up to four weeks to germinate but the germination rate tends to be good, so sowing sparingly will reduce the need to thin out the seedlings when they grow.

Keep pots and trays warm and watered but never waterlogged, in a bright spot in the house or greenhouse. As celery seeds take a while to germinate, it's important not to forget them—make sure the compost doesn't dry out. A light spray of water twice a day is ideal, especially if the pots are in a sunny spot indoors.

If the seedlings are very crowded when they start to grow, gently remove a few and cover up any exposed roots of the remaining plants. Young plants should be kept warm and watered regularly until all danger of a frost has passed.

Planting out

When the young plants are about 10–15 cm. (4–6 in.) high, and the weather has warmed up, they can be put outside. Prepare the ground well in a sunny, well-drained spot in the garden. Dig over and remove any perennial weeds, large stones and non-organic debris. Hoe or rake the soil to a fairly fine consistency.

Celery grown for the stems will need to be "earthed up" later on in the growing year, and as a result it is often planted in trenches to facilitate this process. Celery germinates so well that you may have hundreds of young plants. Some can be planted in trenches to develop into celery stems later, while others can be planted in lines or dotted round the vegetable patch or herb garden for leaves and seeds. Some of the hybrid varieties of celery may not over-winter in your region. These can sometimes be mulched or protected with cloches or alternatively grown in the greenhouse or in containers.

It is essential they get enough water. Allow 15–20 cm. (6–8 in.) between plants if growing in lines and water well after planting. Earthing up should be done as soon as the plants are growing well if you are cultivating the celery for stems. Simply rake up the soil on either side of the plants and cover the stems. As they get bigger, the stems can be tied together loosely with natural twine to stop them flopping outwards. Protect the plants from cold during the winter.

Wild celery (*Apium graveolens*) is hardier and less susceptible to bugs and viruses than the hybrid versions, and it will have more chance of surviving a chilly winter.

Container Growing

Celery will grow readily in containers or large pots. Fill well-drained pots with fresh compost and allow 15–20 cm. (6–8 in.) around each plant. Water your containers well after planting and regularly throughout the summer. Keep your plants in a sunny spot on the patio or balcony. They can be grown indoors as long as they have enough light and water.

Before the first frosts, plants should be brought inside if possible and kept in a sunny spot in the house or warm greenhouse. Keep the pots watered and the plants will not only flower the following year, they may also provide fresh celery leaves throughout the winter months.

Harvesting

All stems should be harvested before the first frost, while the leaves can be used as soon as the plants are growing well. Never strip one plant of all its leaves—take one or two from each plant to encourage more growth. In cold winter regions, hybrid celery plants are more likely to produce seed if grown in containers and kept indoors during the winter.

Gardening Tip

Celery is in the same family of plants as parsley and is related to fennel. To avoid any cross-pollination, it's best to grow celery in the vegetable patch if you have fennel in the herb garden

Using and storing celery

Seeds

When the flower heads have developed seeds, snip these from the plant and hang the flower stems upside down in paper bags in a dry airy place until the seeds drop into the bags. Store in labelled jars and keep out of direct light.

NB: Celery seed bought for cultivation shouldn't be eaten, as they are often treated with fungicides. Wait to eat the seeds produced by your own plants. Celery seed is often crushed and used as a salt to flavor soups and stews. They are used in Ayurvedic medicines to alleviate bronchial complaints and also to treat nervous conditions.

Leaves

Celery leaves can be hung up and dried in sprigs as above, then crumbled into jars when completely dry. Label and store out of direct light. Celery leaf is stronger in taste than the stems and is a useful flavoring for many dishes. Fresh or dried leaves can be added to soups, stews, casseroles, and salads. However, as with most herbs, fresh leaves are usually fuller in taste than dried leaves. Chop fresh leaves before adding to food.

Stems

These can be eaten raw, but are also a staple addition to soups and stews—celery, carrot, and onion are a famous trio in many cuisines.

Coriander

Although coriander isn't mentioned as often as mint and parsley in cookery writing, it is one of the most widely used herbs around the world. It probably originated in southern Europe and parts of Asia, but grows easily in many regions around the world and in some parts, coriander still grows wild. Coriander is officially an annual herb, but in the right environment will reseed and come up year after year in ideal conditions.

Coriander has been around for thousands of years—seeds have been found in tombs dating back 5000 years. It has always been used to flavor food and also used in many medicinal preparations over the centuries. There is evidence that the ancient Greeks and Egyptians used coriander to treat various medical conditions, and some Chinese cultures believed that coriander bestowed immortality.

Fresh coriander leaves add an exotic flavor to any dish and can be added to the salad bowl to spice up a green salad. Seeds are used in sweet dishes as well as savory ones and are said to aid digestion. They can be added to home-baked bread recipes and also used as a pickling spice.

Growing advice

Coriander is always propagated from seed but can take a while to germinate. Seedlings don't transplant well, so seed should always be sown *in situ*. Plants growing in full sun will be encouraged to run to seed quickly and won't produce a lot of foliage. Start seeds in a bright sunny spot if you are growing for seed only but allow the plants a little shade if you want more leaf. A couple of coriander patches in the garden will give you both—a short line of seeds sown in the vegetable patch will come up every year, if the winters aren't too cold. You may find that plants seed themselves and pop up all over the garden; coriander isn't invasive and can be pulled up and used if it is in the way. Make sure the ground is well draining, as plants won't tolerate waterlogged soil.

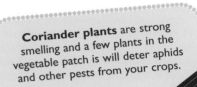

Coriander plants are strong smelling and a few plants in the vegetable patch is will deter aphids and other pests from your crops.

Dig over the ground well and remove any perennial weeds, large stones and non-organic debris. Rake or hoe the soil to a fine consistency. Seeds like a fine soil to germinate, so a well-prepared area is essential for a good germination rate.

Sowing

Seeds should be sown early in spring once any danger of frost has passed; protect with a plastic cover or cloche at night if there is any risk. Sow seed in drills about 1 cm. (½ in.) deep, allowing about 3–5 cm. (1–2 in.) between seeds. The plants will need thinning out later on, and as coriander does not transplant very successfully, the fewer plants that need pulling out the better. Cover seed with fine compost or soil and water gently.

Seeds can also be scattered over a prepared bed and then raked in gently. Do this if you have plenty of seed as they are more vulnerable to birds and other wildlife if left uncovered.

Plant care

Thin out the seedlings when necessary, allowing about 20 cm. (8 in.) between each strong seedling. The plants you remove can be used in the kitchen immediately. Keep young plants watered and weed-free.

Coriander is prolific once it gets going, but young plants are delicate and can be easily strangled by weeds.

When plants begin to flower, pinch flowers off carefully to encourage the plant to produce more leaf. Only those plants grown for the seeds should be allowed to flower and develop seed. Seed can be collected easily by simply placing a cloth or cardboard around the base of the plants to collect it as it falls.

Collected seed can be used in the kitchen and also stored to sow next year in the garden. Germination rates may be a little more erratic with "home-produced" seed, therefore sow more than you would normally.

Water plants regularly, especially in very dry weather and provide a little shade if you want to keep foliage production going. If plants look tired or are not thriving, it could be that the soil is poor. Feed with an organic feed if necessary but be careful not to use any other type of chemical feed as this will affect the taste of the leaves.

Container Growing

Coriander grows well in pots and containers that are well-drained and filled with fresh compost. As the seedlings don't transplant well, sow a few in each pot, and keep one or two plants to grow on, depending on the size of the pot.

Seeds can be sown in biodegradable pots and then the whole pot planted in a larger container later. Be careful not to damage roots and water well after planting. Keep pots in a sunny spot, although a little shade is necessary for leaf production. Coriander plants will often thrive on a sunny windowsill. Don't forget to water them.

Coriander is a fairly hardy plant, especially once over the seedling stage, and doesn't tend to be vulnerable to bugs or viruses. It can, however, "bolt" or run to seed too quickly if the plants are getting too much sun. A little shade from the midday sun will help avoid bolting.

Using and storing coriander

Seeds
Once collected, coriander seeds can be stored for many months without losing flavor. Allow the seeds to dry for a day or two before storing in glass jars and keep out of direct light. Save some to sow next year in case the winter is too harsh for your plants to have reseeded outside. Seeds can be used as a pickling spice. Bruise them before putting into vinegar for pickling vegetables. Coriander seeds are also used in Asian cooking, and make an appearance in many curry spice mixtures. Coriander is believed to aid digestion and the seeds are used in preparations to alleviate rheumatic pain.

Leaves
The leaves can be dried successfully and stored for a few months before they start to lose their flavor. Hang sprigs upside down in paper bags then crumble into glass jars. Label and store out of direct light. Some people have had success quick-freezing the leaves. Add fresh and dried leaves to stews, casseroles and curry dishes to give a spicy fresh flavor. Fresh chopped leaves are also wonderful in tomato salsas, guacamole, and in Thai dishes.

Fennel

Fennel is a versatile plant. Not only are the seeds used as a spice and the leaves used as an herb, the bulb of the plant is used as a vegetable. However, plants grown for their leaves and seeds or wild varieties won't often produce a swollen bulb, so buy hybrid seeds to produce fennel bulbs.

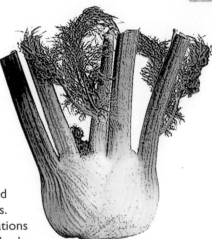

Although indigenous to Mediterranean regions, fennel is now grown widely around the world and will tolerate cooler climates. Fennel has been used in medicinal preparations for many centuries: it was one of the few herbs revered by the Anglo-Saxons, and the ancient Greeks believed it to be a helpful slimming aid, which recent research seems to be supporting. It aids digestion and stimulates the appetite, resulting in less grazing and fewer calories consumed.

The plant often reseeds itself and is sometimes considered to be a perennial plant. It is always biennial, producing foliage in the first year and flowers and seed in the second year of growth. Fennel grown for bulbs alone are grown as annual plants.

Fennel plants will repel certain insects and in medieval times, it was believed to protect against witches. The powerful chemical constituents of fennel can sometimes have an effect on the growth of other plants so it is best planted in its own space.

Growing advice

Fennel is propagated from seed and is one of the easiest herbs to grow for its leaves and seeds. To develop a swollen root vegetable, hybrid seeds should always be used and growing recommendations checked before sowing. Plants will need earthing up later in the year to "blanch" the stem and produce the fennel bulb.

To grow fennel for its leaves or seeds is easy enough even for the most inexperienced gardener. However, keep in mind that during hot sunny periods, plants can bolt and also cause other crops growing nearby to do the same. In some cases, the presence of fennel will cause other plants to die back completely. Tomatoes and beans, in particular, should not be grown nearby. Fennel plants grown in a very sunny spot should be shaded from the midday sun until they are growing well.

Sowing

Seeds can be sown directly outside, but not until later in the spring; they should be protected with a cloche or similar cover at night until all danger of frost has passed. Prepare the ground to a fine consistency, sow seed sparingly and water carefully. Keep soil watered but not waterlogged, and weed-free. When the seedlings are about 5 cm. (2 in.) high, thin out to allow about 30 cm. (12 in.) of space per plant. Seedlings removed won't transplant well, but they can be used in the kitchen.

Fennel doesn't transplant easily, so if seed is sown early in the year it should be sown in biodegradable pots so the whole pot can be planted out later on. Sow sparingly in biodegradable pots of fresh compost and keep warm and watered until all danger of frost has passed. Then plant out in an area away from other crops in a semi-shady position. Prepare the ground first. Dig over the soil and remove any perennial weeds and large stones. Fennel plants grown only for the bulb will need a better depth of prepared soil. Fennel doesn't thrive in heavy soil, so add some sand or other soil conditioner before planting if your soil tends to be on the heavy side. Check the manufacturer's recommendations on your seed packet.

Planting on

After planting, water well and keep weeds away. Fennel grows fairly well with dill, which is biologically similar, but avoid growing near coriander if planting in the herb garden (see page 28 for its ill effects on other plants). Position behind lower-growing plants to avoid over shadowing. Fennel plants should be spaced at least 30 cm. (12 in.) apart to allow for growing room. (Check your seed packet for variety or regional differences.)

Container Growing

Fennel can be grown in containers although plants can grow quite tall, so may need support or to be positioned against a fence or wall. Sow seed directly in well-drained containers or large pots of fresh compost and keep warm and watered. Don't let the soil dry out and shade from the midday sun in very hot periods.

Fennel bulbs will only tolerate a light frost or two and all plants should be dug up before a prolonged cold spell. However, the fennel herb is biennial and will produce flowers and seeds during its second year of growth so should be left in the ground to mature. A light fleece or other protection may be necessary if the winter is extremely cold, but generally fennel plants are fairly hardy and will survive the cold weather once established.

Use leaves from your plants as soon as they are growing well. Take a few leaves from each plant to encourage them to produce more.

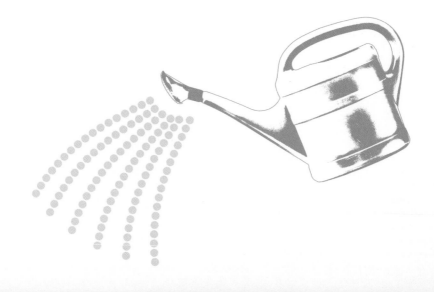

Using and storing fennel

Seeds

Fennel seed heads can be collected from the plant before they are fully mature and hung upside down in paper bags in a dry airy place until the seeds drop out into the bag. Store in labelled glass jars out of direct light. Seeds can be used in the kitchen in various recipes, and can also be sown the following spring for next year's crop. Fennel (especially fennel tea made from seeds) is a very effective digestive aid and can relieve flatulence problems. It is also considered to be a useful herb for increasing milk flow in nursing mothers, as well as helping to treat ailments such as sore throats and gum disease.

Leaves

The feathery leaves are best used fresh if possible but they can be dried or frozen if necessary. Freeze quickly or dry by hanging sprigs as above until leaves can be crumbled into a jar for storing. Fennel leaves have a great affinity with fish, particularly oily fish. The leaves can also be chopped and added to salads.

Nasturtiums

Nasturtiums are very practical, pretty plants to grow, especially in a cottage garden, where they will sprawl over empty spaces and attract good insects to the vegetable patch. Flowers and leaves grow from a trailing vine, which can be trained to cover a fence or used as ground cover. Both flowers and leaves are edible, having a peppery taste similar to watercress.

This herb and spice has been cultivated for centuries: the leaves are used in salads as well as soups and stews while the seeds are an ideal alternative to capers and are used in pickling. The flowers are also edible and can be used as a garnish.

In milder climates, nasturtiums will reseed themselves and come up year after year. Although a good ground cover plant, it isn't particularly invasive and is easy to remove if necessary.

The flowers attract bees and frogs to the garden. Frogs love the shady environment created by the foliage and will in turn demolish the slugs in the vegetable patch. Position nasturtiums on a corner of the vegetable plot for best companion planting.

Growing advice

In colder climates, nasturtiums may need to be planted every year. Seeds can be collected to sow the following spring. Nasturtium bedding plants are often available at garden centres and are a good way to get started, however, plants may need hardening off for a few days before putting out, especially if there is a possibility of frost. Put outside during the day and bring in at night until night temperatures are warmer, when the plants can be planted out into the garden. Prepare the ground well, removing any weeds and set the plants about 30 cm. (12 in.) apart. Container-grown plants can be set a little closer.

Sowing

Nasturtiums germinate successfully from seeds and there are a number of hybrid varieties available. For best results use the *Tropaeolum majus* species, which is hardier than some hybrids and also has a stronger-tasting leaf.

Buy seed from a reputable manufacturer. With a little luck, you may never have to buy them again, so starting off with the best possible seeds will pay dividends in the long run. Check on the seed packet for recommended sowing times in your region. Generally nasturtium seed is sown in late spring directly outside or in containers.

In mid to late spring, prepare soil for sowing seeds. Dig over and remove any perennial weeds and large stones, then rake or hoe to a fine consistency. Very rich soil will produce more foliage than flowers. To get a fairly even balance don't dig in any compost or well-rotted manure before sowing, unless soil is very poor.

Seed should be sown in shallow drills, placing one seed every 20–25 cm. (8–10 in.) along the line. To grow nasturtiums with your vegetables or in the herb garden, sow a few seeds in well-prepared soil on a corner of the bed or in a pre-designed area. Mark the area with a stick or something similar and remember to water regularly until seeds germinate. Nasturtiums like a sunny well-drained spot in the garden but don't like to dry out completely. Use as ground cover or sow along the border of a lawned area in the garden.

Seeds can be started earlier by using biodegradable pots and kept warm until large enough to plant out. Plant the whole pot out to avoid damaging the roots. Pots should be soaked in water first and the ground prepared well before planting.

Container growing

Nasturtiums grow well in containers but do trail and can grow quite large. Allow about 20 cm. (8 in.) between plants or grow in individual pots or containers.

Because of their trailing flowers and bright foliage, nasturtiums are an attractive hanging basket plant. Baskets must be well drained, never allowed to dry out and positioned in a sunny spot. In ideal conditions, they will produce a wonderful edible display for many months of the year.

Add a nasturtium plant to containers of fruit and vegetable crops to encourage bees to your plants.

Planting on

When plants are growing well, leaves can be used as and when required, although plants should never be stripped of all their leaves. Taking one or two at a time from each plant will encourage them to develop more. The same applies to the flowers. Nasturtium plants can flower for many months of the year, sometimes up until the first frost of winter.

Nasturtium is a vine and as well as being excellent ground cover, it can be trained to climb over a trellis. Set up the structure before planting or sowing seeds so as not to damage the plants and roots later on.

Using and storing nasturtiums

Seed

As soon as the flowers start to die back, place a cloth on the soil around your plants to collect seed. Seed can be collected to plant next year or for use in the kitchen. In milder winter regions, seed left to fall will germinate in the following spring.

Seed should be completely dry before storing. Keep in airtight jars out of direct light to retain the flavor. Seeds can be sown the following year or used in pickling spices and other recipes. Nasturtium seeds are an inexpensive alternative to capers. They have anti-bacterial properties and can help treat minor skin conditions and respiratory problems.

Flowers and leaves

Flowers stay fresh for just a few hours and don't store well so use immediately to garnish salads. Leaves stay edible for a couple of days in the salad compartment of the fridge. Use chopped fresh leaves in mixed green salads, and garnish with a flower or two. Leaves are high in vitamin C and also have a place in treating minor skin conditions.

Herbs

There are many herbs that can be grown at home, although some may need extra care if you live in a cooler climate and are trying to grow plants that like the heat. This chapter outlines some common herbs that can be grown in almost any climate, and with care, all will thrive in the right environment and conditions. One of the most important conditions for herbs is good drainage.

Aloe vera

Aloe vera is thought to have originated in Africa but will grow well in many habitats around the world. A perennial evergreen succulent producing long spear-shaped leaves, it grows to 30 cm. (12 in.) high indoors but can grow significantly higher in warmer outdoor climates. Plants also spread so care should be taken to replant in large enough pots.

There is evidence that aloe vera has been used in medicinal preparations for over 2000 years, and that continues to this day with an explosion of products containing aloe vera, including soaps, detergents and face creams. It is also processed into health drinks and juices. Scientific research has proved that aloe vera has many healing properties—gels from aloe vera are used as a skin treatment after radiotherapy to help the healing process.

Aloe vera is an unusual herb in that it continues to absorb carbon dioxide at night while releasing oxygen. This means that if you have a sunny bedroom, it's perfectly safe to keep your aloe vera plants there both day and night.

The sap from inside the large leaves is the most nutritious part of the plant although in commercial processing it is usual to use the whole leaf. At present, it's not considered wise to consume the outer parts of the leaf.

Growing advice

Aloe vera will tolerate very high and very low temperatures, but it won't survive low ground temperatures. If you live in a region prone to frost, it's best to grow aloe vera in a container that you can bring in during the winter or keep indoors all year round in cool temperate climates. It can be grown indoors right through the year as long as it has light and warmth, and it it doesn't mind if you forget to water it occasionally!

Propagation from offshoots

The best way to start aloe vera is with offshoots from a larger established plant. Given the right conditions, a plant will produce five or six of these offshoots every year and will repot easily. If you can't find someone with offshoots to give away, start by buying a healthy plant from a garden centre or your local garden supplier. These plants are often in pots that are too small for them so repot as soon as you can.

Once you have a few offshoots, fill well-drained pots with good potting compost and plant the shoots carefully but firmly. If the compost is damp, water sparingly and gently to allow the plant to become established. Then allow the compost to dry out totally before watering again. Use pots large enough to allow for growing room. Sand can be mixed with compost to help with drainage if you feel the compost is a little on the heavy side.

Keep plants in a warm place. A sunny windowsill is ideal although care should be taken that the leaves don't get scorched through the glass. In warmer climates, aloe vera can be planted outside in well-drained soil. Mature plants grown outdoors may produce seed and grow much larger than container-grown or inside plants. Collect the seed if you can to start off a new crop.

If you have success with your first aloe vera plants, it's a good idea to allow some more space for them the following year.

Propagation by seed

Aloe can be started from seed although germination may be slow—anything from one to six months is usual. Sow seeds in well-drained trays or pots of fresh compost and don't exclude light, as the seeds require light to germinate. Keep compost damp until germinated then water about once a week, depending on the heat and airflow. Again, some sand could be mixed with the compost before sowing seed.

Planting on

Plants tend to grow very quickly and will need repotting to larger containers about once a year. If the plant is healthy and has produced offshoots, these will need to be repotted anyway. Shake the plant out of its pot carefully and the smaller plants will easily fall away from the "mother" plant. Replant straight away. If any of the shoots have damaged roots, leave them to dry out for an hour or two and then repot. Healthy roots though will undoubtedly grow better plants.

Although aloe vera is indigenous to hotter climates, it doesn't respond well to humidity, so a windowsill is ideal for airflow if you are growing indoors. Plants can be fed with an organic food every so often, although aloe vera is generally able to thrive in even the poorest of soils.

Container Growing

Aloe vera thrives well in properly drained containers but will need repotting every year. If the soil you are using is a little tired you may want to feed the plants a couple of times during the spring and summer months. As mentioned above, allow the pots to dry out before watering. If the top couple of inches of soil feels dry, it's time to water.

Keep pots or containers in a sunny or bright spot in the house with plenty of airflow. During hot summer months, containers could be placed outside, but don't leave them out on a cold night.

Using and storing aloe vera

Aloe vera will survive all year in the right environment and shouldn't need any storing at all; simply take leaves as you need them.

Aloe vera has a number of amino acids that help to repair damaged skin and it is the basis of a soothing gel for sunburn. It is also considered to have anti-ageing properties and has been used for centuries to soothe certain stomach disorders. Research is still going on to discover all the medicinal qualities of this plant, but good results have been reported concerning its skin-healing properties in conditions such as eczema.

Always consult your doctor before taking aloe preparations if you have a medical condition and/or are taking medications in case there are contra-indications. Peel the leaf as thinly as possible to remove the outer layer, then gently apply the inside of the leaf to the affected area. The cooling effect is immediate.

Basil

Although native to Asia and the Middle Eastern countries, basil has been grown widely across Europe for many centuries. There is evidence that basil has been used as a culinary and medicinal herb for thousands of years. These days we tend to think of basil as the "tomato" herb because nothing enhances the flavor of tomatoes quite like basil.

Legendary Herb

Many myths and legends have attached themselves to basil over the centuries, including the belief that basil opened the gates to heaven. It was once thought that a sprig of basil worn in the hair would attract a loved one, as it was believed to be the herb of love and purity.

In warmer climates basil grows as a biennial, producing flower and seed during the second year of growth. In cooler climates, however, basil is nearly always grown as an annual plant. There are a number of hybrid seed varieties available with different leaf colours as well as different tastes and some varieties taste of lemon or lime. Choose your seeds carefully and you could have a wonderful herbal display with lots of different flavors on your kitchen windowsill.

Growing advice

Although basil will grow outdoors in cooler climates, the seed shouldn't be sown directly outside until the air and soil temperatures have warmed up and after all danger of frost has passed. Buy good-quality seed from a reputable supplier to get the best possible crops.

Propagation by seed

The best way to start your seeds is in a warm place in early spring. Sow in well-drained pots or trays of fresh compost and keep the soil damp but never waterlogged. Keep pots on a sunny windowsill or in a warm greenhouse or conservatory, and protect from cold drafts until seedlings appear. Keep warm and watered until the plants are large enough to handle and have at least four or five true leaves.

Planting out

Repot individual plants into well-drained larger pots filled with good potting compost. Keep pots indoors in a sunny place and water regularly. After all danger of frost has passed basil can be put outside.

Either repot plants into fairly large pots to grow on or plant directly into the herb garden or vegetable patch. Choose a sunny spot as basil likes at least five hours of sun every day if possible.

> **Gardener's Tip**
>
> It's a good idea to place a couple of basil plants with your tomatoes so you won't forget to pick it.

Prepare the ground beforehand by digging over and removing any perennial weeds and large stones. Rake to a fine consistency, especially if you are sowing seed directly outside. Basil plants aren't heavy feeders and will tolerate fairly poor soil. Check on your seed packet for the manufacturer's growing instructions, but generally you should allow about 30 cm. (12 in.) or more for each plant to grow into.

Although the strong scent of basil tends to deter flies and pests, it isn't immune to slug attacks. Protect your plants by spreading crushed eggshells around the base of each stem or use any other preferred organic slug repellent.

When the flower heads start to grow, pinch off the whole branch and the plant will produce more foliage. In warmer climates, leave in the ground outside or in containers, and the plants will produce flower and seed the following year. To collect seed, either hang stems upside down in paper bags to catch them, or place a cloth or card around the plant as soon as the flowers start producing seed.

As soon as the plant has become established and is growing well, pick leaves regularly to encourage more growth, although never strip an entire plant. If possible, grow two or three plants and pick a few leaves from each plant when required.

Container growing

Basil grows well in containers and pots (see pages 41–42 for sowing and growing advice). Keep in a sunny or bright spot and don't let the soil dry out. If kept warm and watered, basil will often carry on growing right into the autumn and will stay fresh and green for picking through to midwinter. In warmer climates, basil will be available practically all year round. Keep a pot of basil near an open window or door to deter flies during the summer months.

Using and storing basil

Add basil leaves to any tomato dish or snack. Chop or tear the leaves and sprinkle over a dish, or stir in just at the end of the cooking time to preserve its flavor. A leaf or two can be an attractive garnish for homemade tomato soups. Basil is considered to be a digestive aid, and some herbalists use it to help cure headaches, constipation and sickness.

Although best used fresh, basil can be stored successfully. Either freeze fresh sprigs quickly and store in the freezer or hang small bunches up to dry in an airy room until the leaves crumble when touched. Hang in paper bags to keep in the scent and flavor as well as saving any leaves from dropping to the floor. Crumble the dried leaves into labeled jars and store out of direct sunlight.

Being picky

Herbs thrive when picked so the more you pick them, the more they will grow! A few leaves will add flavor and depth to many different dishes.

Bay

An evergreen shrub native to Europe and parts of Asia, bay will grow into a huge tree rather than a shrub if left to its own devices in an ideal environment. Generally bay is grown in tubs or large planters to keep it under control.

A respected and ancient herb, bay was used to make garlands or headdresses to adorn noblemen or the victors in battle—its botanical name *Laurus nobilis* roughly translated means "noble laurel." Bay was used medicinally at one time as it has strong antiseptic properties and it has always been used as a culinary herb; bay is one of the main ingredients, along with parsley and thyme, in *bouquet garnis*, a collection of herbs added to many recipes.

Growing advice

Bay is a hardy woody shrub and is generally propagated by layering or taking cuttings. It is possible to grow using seed but germination tends to be poor and will take some time. If you are going to go down this route, buy seed from a good supplier and check on the manufacturer's sowing recommendations. Generally seed should be sown in containers on moist compost with a layer of dry compost over them. Keep in a dark warm place until seedlings appear.

In an ideal environment your bay tree may produce fruit. The fruits aren't edible but the seeds inside can be collected and sown. Bay isn't susceptible to pests and disease and its worst enemies are cold and water-logging. Always make sure bay is in a well-drained sunny position in the garden, protected from draughts and frosts. In very cold regions, bay can be grown in containers and brought indoors during the winter. Spray the plant from time to time with water and avoid drying too much in a centrally heated home.

Propagation by cuttings

Fill a fairly large pot or well-drained container with fresh compost in the autumn. Prune an existing bay tree and keep cuttings that have a "heel," a side shoot attached to the stem, if possible. Strip the leaves to three or four at most and push the cut end into the pot of compost. The cut end of the stem can be dipped in a hormonal product to speed up the root growth but this isn't absolutely necessary. Plant as many as you have space for since they may not all develop roots.

Once planted the container or pot must be kept in the dark until the new plants have developed. For success, the higher the humidity the better—a heated greenhouse is ideal but the pot must be kept dark. Repot individual plants when they are growing well. Don't use any of the leaves until the plants have been re-potted and grown on for a few weeks.

Propagation by layering

Find a low-growing healthy branch from an established plant and hoe or gently dig the soil where the branch naturally touches the ground. Then push the branch into the soil and secure with a plastic U-shaped peg or something similar (see illustration below of rosemary being layered). Sprinkle some rich seed or potting compost on top of the pegged part of the stem and water gently.

Keep watered and weed-free until the branch has produced roots and a new plant has begun to grow. Once established, this new plant can be replanted elsewhere and the rest of the unused branch cut from the original plant.

Planting out

Bay can be grown outside in a sunny sheltered position in many regions. It is probably advisable to contain the root growth if possible. Because they can grow so large, the roots take many nutrients from the ground that may be better left to feed your other crops or plants. Bay produces plenty of foliage and unless you are growing it commercially, a small plant will usually be plenty for an average family.

Always make sure your bay trees get water even if they are growing outside. They are generally in a sunny position so will dry out quickly if grown in containers or if there is little rainfall.

Container Growing

Bay is often grown in containers to restrict its roots. The shrubs can be shaped and their roots will tolerate a tight squeeze for some time before they need repotting, possibly up to five years.

The main reason why bay plants die in containers is through lack of water. The soil should be moist, never waterlogged. The leaves start to go brown at the edges when the plant needs water, but a regular watering will keep them thriving.

Perfect Presents

Bay trees make a lovely gift and are an attractive feature on a patio or balcony. Start a few cuttings in the autumn months and look after them for a year and you could have your Christmas present list organized.

Using and storing bay

Bay is evergreen, although a few dried leaves can be kept in a sealed glass jar for use in the winter months if your plants struggle through the cold weather. Simply pick them off the plant, dry carefully then pop them into a jar where they will last for about a year before losing their flavor.

In the past, bay has been used in external medicinal preparations as an antiseptic and to ease rheumatic pain. These days, bay is an important part of many different cuisines and adds flavor to stocks, stews, and casseroles. Bay also adds an interesting note to stewed apples and pears, and is often used in pickling.

Chives

Chives originate from Europe, Asia and North America and grow happily in most parts of the world. They have been collected from the wild for many centuries but weren't cultivated specifically until the Middle Ages. They still grow wild in many parts of Europe and North America.

A member of the allium or onion family, chives don't have the powerful taste or medicinal properties of ordinary onions, but it is an easy herb to grow and will come up year after year in the right environment. In many places chives remain green throughout the year, while in cooler climates it's possible to keep them growing through the winter on a bright windowsill, as long as it is not too cold.

Chives produce purple or white flowers that are also edible and make an attractive salad garnish. There are a number of different hybrid varieties available to grow from seed, including garlic chives, sometimes called Chinese chives.

Chives are an attractive border plant for your herb garden and look great dotted around the vegetable garden. They always look particularly fresh and appetizing so use them!

Growing advice

Most plants in the onion family, such as onions or shallots, are difficult to get started from seed, but chives are the exception to the rule. The seed usually germinates well but always buy from a reputable supplier and check the growing recommendations. Chives are resistant to many pests and viruses, but they are susceptible to onion fly. To avoid this, simply plant chives as far as you can from your onion crops; positioning them close to other crops will help deter pests from the vegetable patch.

Propagation by seed

Fill well-drained pots or trays with fresh compost and sow seeds by shaking them sparingly over the surface of the damp compost. Cover with a very fine layer of dry compost and then water using a mister or light water sprayer. Keep the pots or containers watered gently but regularly so that the compost doesn't dry out. Keep in a warm place to encourage seeds to germinate.

Allow the seedlings to grow for a few weeks before planting out in the garden or repotting. They shouldn't be put out too early as a sharp overnight frost could kill them. Keep small plants in pots for the first year before putting out into the garden to help them develop strong roots. Chives will survive a cold winter once they are larger and stronger.

Before planting in the garden, choose a sunny spot, dig over the ground, and remove any large stones and perennial weeds. Hoe or rake to a fine consistency. Plant out in the evening if possible to let them settle overnight. Keep watered and weed-free and your chive plants will thrive.

Propagation by root division

Root division can be done using an existing established plant. As long as the plant has been growing for two or three years, the root system will be large enough to divide.

Dig up the whole plant during the early spring or autumn months. Use a fork and loosen the soil in a fairly large area around the plant. It may help to water the ground first if it's too dry. The most important thing is not to damage the roots too much. When the whole plant has been removed from the soil, separate the roots into two or more pieces. Pull apart gently but firmly, keeping damage to the roots at a minimum.

Replant the pieces as soon as possible and water in well. Spread a layer of mulch over the new plants during the winter if the temperature is very low. Remove as soon as the chives start shooting again.

Growing on

By dividing your larger plants every year, it's possible to create whole borders of chives, perhaps around a small lawn area of the garden or around the vegetable patch. Pots of chives make good gifts, especially as they stay green throughout the winter.

Plants grown outside may die back during the winter, but will send up new shoots in the spring. Mulch over the tops of the plants if the winter is very cold. Plants tolerate fairly poor soil, but if your chives aren't thriving, it may be that the soil is too poor in nutrients. Feed with an organic feed every couple of weeks during the summer to get them growing again.

Harvesting

Use scissors to harvest chives and cut from the outside of the plant inwards so that the outer leaves regenerate as you progress to the centre of the plant. After flowering, cut right down to a couple of inches high and they will grow again.

Container Growing

Chives are perfect herbs for containers, and can be grown on a bright windowsill indoors. Plants will often stay green and usable right through the winter. Otherwise they can be planted in fairly large pots or containers and placed in a sunny spot on the patio or balcony or scattered around the garden. Their purple or white flowers create a wonderful display for weeks.

If their location gets very hot, it may be best to shade chives a little from the midday sun.

Always make sure pots or containers are watered regularly and that they are well drained. When the plants get too big for the pots, separate by root division (see page 48) and repot immediately.

Using and storing chives

A pot of chives indoors will probably stay green all year, however, if you are growing outside and have a cold winter, it is possible to freeze chives. Cut small bunches and freeze quickly. Label and store in the freezer. Use until the fresh ones are available again.

Chives can be cut into small pieces with scissors or chopped and added to fresh potato salads, green salads, and more or less any sandwich where a hint of onion is wanted. They can also be used as a garnish for soups or other dishes. Chopped chives are a welcome addition to yoghurt-based sauces such as tzatziki. The flowers are edible and can also be added to the salad bowl.

Lavender

One of the best-loved
and well-known herbs,
lavender is grown all over
the world. It's a hardy
perennial and given the
right environment and
conditions, will live for
many years. Often found
growing over stone walls in rural
areas, this fragrant herb can be used to
separate different areas of your garden.

Lavender has been used as a medicinal and culinary herb for centuries.
Lavender water was considered to be a useful remedy for fainting,
headaches, and nausea, while an essential oil extracted from the flowers is
used in many cosmetic preparations and in products such as soaps,
detergents and air fresheners.

For many years, lavender was added to food to help calm the stomach.
It has also been used in ointments and other medicinal preparations in the
ancient world: the ancient Greeks used it to treat insect bites as well as
stomach disorders, while the ancient Egyptians placed it in the tombs of
royalty. The flowers are particularly attractive to bees—some of which
produce a high-quality honey—and butterflies, both of which help
pollination, leading to healthier crops around the garden.

Growing advice

Lavender shrubs will continue to grow for up to thirty years given the
right conditions, so choose a sunny, well-drained spot. Lavender grows well
on stone walls and in raised beds, but as long as the ground is well-drained
it can be grown just about anywhere. It prefers a light soil that is not too
acidic; if yours is acidic, add a little lime before you plant lavender to give it
a good start.

A hardy shrub, lavender can grow 15–100 cm. (6–40 in.) or more depending on the variety and environment. Lavender can be started from cuttings or from seed but germination tends to be a bit erratic. Buy seed from a good supplier and check the sowing recommendations on the seed packet before you start.

Container Growing

Lavender can be successfully grown in containers. Make sure they are well drained and filled with fresh organic compost. Don't use acidic soil in containers. Keep containers in a sunny spot outside on a patio or balcony and water sparingly from time to time. However, lavender is best grown outside in open ground, so keep an eye on the moisture level if growing in a container or pot, and note how healthy your plants are before watering.

Propagation by seed
Generally seed should be sown in well-drained trays or pots of fresh compost. Keep in a warm greenhouse or a bright place in the house, and water from time to time. Never let the compost become too wet. When the seedlings are large enough to handle, repot or put out in the garden.

The ground should be dug over and any perennial weeds removed. Incorporate lime if your soil is on the acidic side. Hoe or rake to a fine consistency, especially if you are putting out very young plants.

Although lavender is a hardy plant and will tolerate cold winters, the seedlings aren't strong enough to survive very cold temperatures. Wait until all danger of frost has passed before planting out in the garden and water sparingly.

When the first year's flowers appear, cut them down to encourage more growth in the rest of the plant. Leaving them to grow may result in a weaker, spindly plant. After the first year lavender should be used as required and will benefit from being cut from time to time.

Propagation from cuttings
The easiest way to propagate lavender is from cuttings. These should be cut from a well-established healthy plant in late summer or early autumn, after the plant has finished flowering. Cut 10–15 cm. (4–6 in.) lengths from healthy stems, preferably with a heel and push into prepared well-

drained pots or containers of fresh compost. In mild winter areas these cuttings could be put straight into a seed bed. Some growers prefer to dip the cut end of the cuttings into a hormone powder to encourage root growth, although this isn't always necessary.

Keep trays or pots warm and watered sparingly until the cuttings have developed roots and are large enough to be repotted or put out in the garden.

Growing on

If a very cold winter is expected, mulch can be layered around the plants to protect the roots from extreme frosts. However, it's essential that the ground isn't too wet before mulching, as the extra moisture kept in the soil may damage the roots. Mulch should be removed in the spring before the plants start to grow again.

If plants become straggly, they can be cut to shape in late summer or early autumn. Lavender, like most herbs, likes to be used and cutting regularly will encourage more growth. English Lavender (*Lavandula angustifolia*) is more tolerant of cold winters but, as stated above, mulch if you are expecting very cold temperatures, especially around plants that are only a year or two old.

Using and storing lavender

The uses of lavender could take up an entire book. Put a sprig or two in drawers to freshen your clothes. A well-known sleep remedy can be made by sewing three sides of two small muslin squares of cotton together to form a bag and fill with crumbled lavender leaves, then sew up the last side of the square. Place under the pillow for a restful night. These lavender bags can also be made for drawers and to give away as gifts.

Lavender is often available throughout the year so needs little storing. The flowers, however, will only last until late summer or autumn, depending on the variety and your region, so should be harvested and stored if required. Store in jars or paper bags out of direct light.

Lemon balm

A hardy perennial shrub, lemon balm (*Melissa officinalis*) has been an important healing herb for thousands of years. Growing to about 60 cm. (2 ft.) high, lemon balm generally dies back in the winter and can become invasive in the garden if not checked.

Native to southern Europe and the Mediterranean regions, lemon balm is grown all over the world. This is a worthy plant to have in your herb garden and it will grow in containers if you haven't space in the garden.

It is best grown along pathways or where the leaves will be brushed against and bruised, releasing its refreshing lemony scent. The attractive foliage makes it a decorative plant to have around the house.

Ancient Remedies

In the Middle Ages, lemon balm was believed to bestow eternal youth and was grown commercially. During the seventeenth century lemon balm was an important ingredient in the medicinal preparation Carmelite water, which was created and produced by Carmelite monks and nuns. Used as an eau de cologne as well as a cordial, Carmelite water was said to alleviate headaches and neuralgia symptoms.

Lemon balm has calming effects due to its mild sedative properties, and is often helpful in treating anxiety disorders. Lemon balm tea with a little honey, and perhaps a sprig of thyme, can be used to alleviate cold symptoms.

Growing advice

Lemon balm can be propagated in a number of ways including from seed, cuttings or from root division.

Propagation by seed

Buy your seed from a good supplier and check the recommendations on the packet. Generally seed can be sown in spring or autumn, however, lemon balm seed can take some time to germinate so a little patience is needed. Sow seeds in well-drained pots or trays of fresh compost and keep warm, or keep in a cold frame until the seedlings are large enough to handle. Birds are attracted to the seed, so protect your pots from birds at all times. Compost should be slightly damp but never too moist.

When the seedlings are large enough to handle, repot into individual pots and protect them until at least 15 cm. (6 in.) high before putting out in the garden. Choose a sunny spot with some shade during the day and prepare the ground well by digging over and removing any perennial weeds and large stones. Hoe or rake to a fairly fine consistency before planting out small plants. Allow about 30 cm. (12 in.) of space between each plant. Double-check the growing recommendations on your seed packet as different varieties may have different spacing requirements.

Propagation from cuttings

Lemon balm propagates well from cuttings. In the autumn, cut 7–10 cm. (3–4 in.) stems from a healthy established plant. These cuttings should then be pushed cut-end down in pots of fresh compost or straight out in the garden. The ground should be prepared as for a seed-bed (as fine a consistency as you can make it). In regions with very cold winters, the young cuttings will need protection from frosts during the first year. If this is the case, it is advisable to set your cuttings in large pots that can be brought inside if you are expecting cold weather.

Not all cuttings will develop roots so plant more than you need. Water regularly if kept indoors but never allow pots to become waterlogged. Lemon balm is fairly drought-resistant so don't over-water, although if kept in a centrally heated house, the pots may dry out quickly.

Planting on

In the following summer, your cuttings should have developed roots. Discard the ones that haven't and replant the ones with roots. Plant into individual pots for another year and then the following year position them in the garden, in a herb garden area or along a pathway. In milder climates, replant straight away into their permanent position. Choose a sunny spot that gets some shade during the day and your plants will last for many years. Lemon balm can become invasive though so keep an eye on this.

The leaves can be used during the first year, as soon as the cuttings have been replanted and are settling into their new position.

Propagation by root division

Root division is an easy way to propagate lemon balm and will also help keep the plants under control, before they take over the herb garden. When the plant has died back in autumn or before it starts to shoot again in spring, gently fork around the plant when the soil is wet and lift out carefully to avoid damage to the roots.

Gently but firmly separate the root system into two or more clumps depending on the size of the plant and how many new plants you want. These clumps should be replanted as soon as possible after digging up. Repot in large well-drained pots or containers of fresh compost or plant out in prepared ground. Potted plants can be put out in the herb garden the following year. Allow the plants to become established before using.

Beloved of Bees

Keep a large container of lemon balm on a patio or balcony to attract bees and butterflies, and rub the leaves from time to time to release the refreshing lemon scent.

Container Growing

Lemon balm grows well in containers and can be grown indoors as well as outside. As it's a hardy shrub it will thrive in most outdoor climates. Pots can be brought indoors or sheltered from very cold winters but generally lemon balm will cope. The plants are also fairly drought-resistant so won't mind not being watered from time to time. Plants grow well on a windowsill but constant hot sun may scorch the leaves, so a little shade protection may be necessary.

Using and storing lemon balm

Lemon balm has always been an important herb, and with good reason. Make a lemon balm tea at night to relax and induce sleep. Simply place a few leaves in a jug and pour on boiling water. Leave to seep for a few minutes and then sip as soon as it's cool enough to drink.

Use the leaves to soothe insect bites and also to deter mosquitoes—crushed leaves rubbed on the skin are reputed to keep them at bay. Leaves can be dried for use in the winter by hanging sprigs uside down in paper bags in a dry airy place until completely dry. Crumble and store in an airtight jar out of direct light.

Lovage

A hardy perennial herb growing up to 120 cm. (4 ft.) high, sometimes more, lovage is native to the Mediterranean regions but grows as an escapee from cultivation in many places around the world. For centuries it was considered a wonder drug in the herbal world, and was used to treat many medical conditions. The stems can be peeled and eaten raw and the leaves add a distinct celery flavor to stews and casseroles.

Lovage seed is sometimes ground and used in place of celery salt and the plant is still grown commercially as a flavoring. Lovage roots can be dried and used as a peppery spice. The plant contains essential oils that give it a distinct flavor and, although easy to grow and maintain, lovage has gone out of fashion from domestic herb gardens over the past few years. Once established in the herb garden, lovage will return every year for many years. Apart from its culinary and medicinal uses, the heavy scent of lovage will help deter bugs and pests from your garden. Positioned carefully in the garden, this plant requires very little attention to thrive.

Growing advice

Lovage can be propagated from seeds or by root division. Always buy seeds from a reputable supplier and check the manufacturer's growing recommendations for your region before you start.

Propagation by seed

Sow seeds early in the spring in well-drained seed trays or pots and keep in the greenhouse. Use fresh compost and keep trays damp but not too wet. Ensure that the seedlings are kept warm until they are large enough to handle and all danger of frost has passed before putting them out into the garden.

Seeds can also be sown directly into a seed bed when the soil and air temperatures have warmed up. Dig over the ground well and remove any perennial weeds, large stones and any non-organic debris. Rake or hoe the top few inches of soil to a fine consistency, since seed will germinate more readily in a finer soil. Water gently and keep weed-free and watered regularly until seedlings are large enough to replant.

Propagation by root division

Lovage propagates well from root division—choose a healthy well-established plant and loosen the soil around the base of the stem in a fairly large circle then gently dig up the whole plant. This should be done as the plant starts to reshoot inearly spring. Gently pull apart the roots into two or more clumps and replant the clumps with shoots immediately.

Container Growing

Generally, lovage isn't really suitable for container growing as it tends to grow very tall and prefers a deep soil.

However, in a deep well-drained container with nutrients added during the growing season, it may grow well.

Repot every year if grown in containers and use fresh organic compost. Roots can be divided every year when being repotted to propagate more plants. Position lovage containers behind low-growing plants to avoid over-shadowing.

Planting on

For most domestic needs, one or two lovage plants will be plenty so if you have more root clumps or seedlings than you need, try to fit them into spaces in the garden where their bug-repelling qualities will be most appreciated, or they could be potted up and given away.

Lovage plants can grow very tall, so should be positioned in a sunny spot at the back of a herb or flower bed so as not to shade your lower-growing plants. Before planting, prepare the ground to a good depth and incorporate some well-rotted manure or compost. Lovage likes a deep fertile soil. Allow about 60 cm. (2 ft.) for the plant to grow into, but double-check this spacing requirement on your seed packet as varieties differ. If you are propagating by root division, you will know how large the original plant was, so allow the space accordingly.

Keep weed-free and water regularly, especially in dry weather. After the first year, lovage tends to look after itself. However, weeds do take nutrients from the soil, so keeping weeds at bay will help produce healthier plants.

Picking the leaves regularly will encourage the plant to produce more foliage. When the flowers appear, either cut them off to allow the plant to keep on producing leaf, or leave the flowers to develop seed to collect for the kitchen or for planting the following year.

Plants die back in the winter and usually leave a straggly stem or two. It's very tempting to cut this back when tidying up at the end of the summer. However, if you leave it, you may have ladybugs taking up residence, which in turn keep aphids out of your garden.

Lovage will grow on for a few years before the plant gets tired. At that point, dig up and divide the roots and start off some new plants.

Using and storing lovage

Seeds
Lovage seeds can be stored for many months. They can be ground and used as a celery salt substitute in cooking or kept for the following spring to be sown in the garden. Keep seeds in a labelled jar out of direct light.

Leaves
Leaves should be dried by hanging upside down in a dry airy place in paper bags to protect them from dust and to catch any broken leaf. Crumble dried leaves into labelled jars and store out of direct light. The flavor will be retained for many months and dried leaves can be added to soups, stews and casseroles during the winter.

Lovage has been used in a number of medicinal preparations to help aid digestion and to stimulate the appetite. It was also added to bath water to cleanse and deodorize the skin before commercial bath oils and soaps were available.

Lovage stems have been candied in the past, like angelica, but is rarely done today. The roots can be dried gently in a very slow oven for a few hours, then cooled and finely grated or ground to use as a peppery spice. Make sure the roots don't actually cook; keep the oven door slightly ajar and the setting very low.

Marigold

Although there are many different varieties of marigold, the traditional "pot marigold" (*Calendula officinalis*) is the one to include in your herb garden. Other varieties are worth growing but pot marigold contains properties sometimes lost in the hybridization process.

Marigolds were once considered to have magical qualities and were planted all over villages at times of celebration. They were used to flavor and color food and treat various minor medical conditions. They also helped to deter pests from the garden. A few marigold plants around your vegetable patch will result in fewer bugs eating your crops.

The plant is native to southern Europe but has adapted to cooler climates over the centuries and now grows wild in many regions, including temperate zones. It is an annual herb and flowers over a long period during the summer and autumn months. The official Latin name *Calendula* means "through the months," indicating the plant flowers for a longer-than-average time.

Easy to grow and a delight to look at as well as being useful, marigolds are a beautiful herb to add to your herb garden or to brighten up any part of your garden or patio.

Growing advice

Marigolds are easily propagated from seed and can be sown directly outside in prepared soil in late spring. Sow quite sparingly as the seedlings will need thinning out later on. Generally, seed sown slightly earlier will yield a better crop if kept in a greenhouse or warm bright spot until seedlings are large enough to plant out.

Propagation by seed

Sow seed outside after all danger of a frost has passed. The ground should
be in a sunny or semi-shady spot and well drained. Dig over and prepare
as a seed bed, remove any large stones and weeds, and hoe or rake to a
fine consistency. Sow seed as recommended on the seed packet, then
water gently after sowing. Only water again in exceptionally dry conditions
until germination.

Unfortunately, slugs are very partial to young marigold plants, and care
should be taken especially if the seed is sown directly outside. Use any
organic method you can to deter the slugs. Crushed eggshells spread
around the base of the plants will help. Thin plants out when 6–8 cm.
(2½–3 in.) high, to allow for about 15 cm. (6 in.) growing-room, or replant
in various spots around the garden. Always add a few to your vegetable
patch if possible, as the flowers attract the good bugs and repel the bad
ones. Choose a sunny or semi-
shady spot for marigolds. When
sowing varieties other than the
pot marigold (*Calendula officinalis*),
check the suppliers' growing
recommendations on the
seed packet to ensure
you provide the best
conditions for your plants
to thrive.

Sowing seed indoors early in the spring allows more time to get the plants going and it can also be easier to keep the slugs away. Sow in well-drained pots or trays of fresh compost and water gently directly after sowing. Keep trays in a warm bright place in the house, conservatory or warm greenhouse if you have one.

The trays shouldn't need watering again before germination as marigold seed tends to germinate quickly. Allow to grow on, watering if necessary until the seedlings are large enough to handle and all danger of frost has passed before planting outside.

Planting out

Transplant as above into sunny or semi-shady spots around the garden or use as a border herb around a flower bed or lawn. Marigolds help deter bugs from your vegetable crops so always plant a few in the vegetable patch. The French *potager* design is perfect for marigolds. Simply create small patches of vegetable crops and grow marigold plants all around the edges. Not only do the crops get a certain amount of protection but the visual effect is stunning.

Container Growing

Marigolds grow very well in containers or pots. They will also be happy on a bright windowsill in the kitchen if you have the space. Plant seedlings in pots as soon as they are large enough to handle. The plants will need watering two or three times a week, depending on their position. Use well-drained pots of fresh compost to avoid weeds and a little mulch will also help keep weeds down. Don't let pots dry out too much.

Position large pots and containers around the patio, balcony or garden to add a splash of color and use the fresh flower heads in the kitchen as they bloom, to encourage more flowers to develop.

Water about twice a week and keep weeds away. Mulching lightly can help discourage weeds. Remove flower heads as they start to die back to encourage more blooms to develop. A few flowers can be left to mature and develop seeds, which can be collected for sowing the following spring. If seeds are left to fall, they will often survive through the winter and marigold plants will come up on their own the following spring in ideal conditions. Plants can keep flowering right up until the first frost, but will then die off.

Using and storing marigold

There are many effective calendula-based commercial creams and lotions on the market, an indication that marigold really is a great healing herb. Flowers can be used to make homemade preparations, and when rubbed onto a bee or wasp sting, will soothe and alleviate the discomfort. Flowers can also be used to make a soothing tea and petals can be stirred gently into a mixed green salad.

Flowers can be dried and will keep for a few months in a sealed jar out of direct light. Make sure the flowers are completely dry before storing. Either hang stems upside down in paper bags in a dry airy place or use a home dryer. Or if watched carefully, marigold flowers can be dried in a very cool oven with the door open for a few hours.

Infuse the leaves of pot marigold to bathe and soothe sore feet.

Mint

One of the best-known and well-used herbs, mint can be grown in almost
any climate. Mint is a hardy perennial and once sown, very rarely needs
resowing—it can be invasive in the garden and should be contained if
necessary (see illustration below for containment ideas). There are around
a thousand different varieties available, including a very convincing
"chocolate" variety that really smells of chocolate mints. Most varieties
will be just as prolific as the original species and the hybrids such as
peppermint and spearmint are particularly popular. Peppermint is the most
widely grown and can be used in either sweet or savory dishes.

Mint has been used for thousands of years and remains a useful herb to
grow in the garden, although care is needed for it not to take over. And it
has many medicinal and culinary uses, including mint sauce, without which
a roast lamb dinner would be incomplete.

Growing advice

Mint can be propagated easily by seed or by root division from a healthy well-established plant. Seeds germinate fairly quickly with a high success rate. Mint prefers a rich soil, a shady spot in the garden and also likes more moisture than many other herbs, although the ground should never be waterlogged. Hybrid varieties may vary, so check your seed packet for the manufacturer's growing recommendations first.

Propagation by seed

Fill well-drained trays or pots with fresh compost. Mint likes rich soil and won't germinate as well in poor garden soil. Keep trays warm and watered until the seedlings are large enough to handle for repotting. Don't let the compost dry out—keeping trays in partial shade will help retain the moisture.

When plants are large enough to handle, they can be transplanted into well-drained larger pots or containers and as before, it's best to fill with fresh compost so that the roots can take up the nutrients the plants need to thrive.

If your plants are going straight out into the garden or herb garden, wait until all danger of frost has passed before putting them out. Although a hardy perennial, the first year's seedlings won't tolerate frost or a very cold night.

Keeping it in Check

Mint can be an invasive plant and will take over the garden if not contained. One way to do this, while still keeping the mint in your chosen spot, is to dig a fairly big hole, in semi-shade if possible, then sink a broken bucket or similar container into the hole (see illustration opposite). Make sure the bucket has sufficient drainage holes. The bottom could be removed entirely.

Fill the bucket with soil dug out of the hole mixed with a rich compost or well-rotted manure and hoe to a fairly fine consistency. Put the mint plants into the soil in the bucket and water well.

Keep weed-free and watered and allow the plants to become established before using them. Even when contained in the garden, mint can still sometimes escape and find its way elsewhere.

Propagation by root division

Before the plants start shooting in the spring or after they have died back in late autumn, mint can be propagated by root division. Sometimes simply breaking off pieces of the plant and repotting in compost or leaving with the cut end in water for a few weeks can work although to be on the safe side, dig up a clump of a well-established plant carefully to avoid damaging roots as much as possible. Fork gently around the plant to loosen the soil, and remove when the soil is damp for the best results and ease of handling.

Break the roots into two or more pieces and replant immediately into well-drained containers or pots of fresh potting compost. Compost should be rich to allow the plants to take up nutrients since mint doesn't thrive in poor soil. Keep watered and weed-free and allow roots to become established before repotting or using the leaves.

Often mint will come up in the most unlikely places, even in an expanse of lawn. However, the plants will smell delicious when mowed and constant cutting should eventually get rid of them.

Container Growing

Mint is an ideal container herb and can be planted in small pots and kept on a windowsill. Don't place in hot direct sun, however, as the soil will dry out too quickly and the leaves may become scorched through glass.

Keep pots of mint around the house, on the patio or on a balcony. There are a number of different varieties that will flower and also produce a lot of attractive foliage.

Pots and containers must be well-drained and as mint likes a rich soil, plants will benefit from being repotted every year into fresh compost.

Using and storing mint

Mint is used in many commercial products from confectionary to alcoholic drinks, as well as in many medicinal preparations. Mint tea is readily available from supermarkets and is accepted as a healthy alternative to caffeine-laden tea and coffee. To make your own mint tea, simply put a few sprigs of mint in a jug and pour over boiling water. Cover and leave to infuse for about five minutes, strain and drink when cool enough.

Make a simple mint dressing by chopping leaves finely and putting into a small bowl. Pour over a couple of tablespoons of malt vinegar, cover, and leave to infuse for thirty minutes or more to allow the flavors to develop.

Use mint leaves to garnish dishes and add to pot pourri mixtures to freshen the air. Fresh mint can be chopped and added to salads and to yoghurt and chopped cucumber to make an excellent dip.

Mint sprigs can be frozen and stored in the freezer for a few months. Mint also dries successfully. Hang sprigs upside down in a cool airy place, preferably in paper bags. When completely dry, crumble into labelled jars and store out of direct light.

After-dinner Digestive

Mint has been used as a digestive aid for centuries, and it is no accident that we eat and love after-dinner mints at the end of a rich meal.

Oregano

Cultivated around the world, oregano (*Origanum vulgare*) is still collected wild in many parts of Europe. It is a perennial herb and grows as a low bush, making it ideal for growing in borders of flower or vegetable beds. As with many herbs, the strong scent will deter pests from your crops.

Native to southwestern Eurasia and the Mediterranean, it was believed to enhance the flavor of meat from the goats that grazed on it. Oregano is a viable commercial plant and is processed into oil that is used in the cosmetic industry. Some of the main areas of current production are in southern Europe and Mexico—the warmer the region, the more pungent the herb. Oregano will grow well in more northern areas, but the scent and flavor will be less intense than plants grown in higher temperatures and a longer growing season.

Oregano is packed with minerals and vitamins and has been an important healing herb for many centuries going back to ancient times. Just a teaspoon of dried oregano leaf contains about 16 mg. calcium, 0.5 mg. vitamin C and 0.4 mg. iron. Oregano is also known as wild marjoram, and there are many hybrid varieties available.

Growing advice

Oregano is an attractive ground-cover plant and can be useful planted among your other plants—it is a perfect herb to grow among roses or other crops that are susceptible to aphid attacks since its strong scent deters many pests. It is a suitable herb for container growing and also grows well in hanging baskets. Although plants prefer a sunny spot, they shouldn't be allowed to dry out too much. Water regularly and ensure pots are well drained.

Propagation by seed

Oregano seed germinates fairly successfully. Buy seed from a good supplier and check the manufacturer's sowing and growing recommendations before you start. Different varieties and different regions will have slightly different needs.

Generally oregano seeds can be sown fairly early in the year as long as the pots are kept warm. Prepare well-drained pots or trays of fresh compost. Warm the trays up before sowing, then sprinkle a few seeds on the surface of the compost and spray gently with water. Spray the seeds with water two or three times a day until they have germinated. Trays or pots can be kept on a warm windowsill or other bright warm place in the house or greenhouse, but avoid too much direct sun before seeds have germinated.

As soon as the seeds have germinated, reduce watering to keep the compost damp but never wet.

Potting on

When the seedlings are large enough to handle, they can be replanted. If you want to keep the plants in their original pots, remove the weaker plants and leave one plant per pot, unless very large pots were used for sowing seed. Allow enough space for the plant to spread and grow—they can often spread to about 1 mt. (3½ ft.) wide. Generally one plant per pot is sufficient.

Planting out

Seedlings that are to be planted outside should be kept warm and watered until all danger of frost has passed. Prepare the soil in a sunny well-drained spot. Dig over, remove any perennial weeds and large stones and rake or hoe to a fine consistency. When the soil has warmed up in late spring, plant out oregano allowing at least 60 cm. (24 in.) between plants. Water after planting and try not to let plants dry out too much, but never water in wet weather or if the soil is already damp. Originally a mountain plant, oregano needs good drainage. When the conditions are right, oregano will thrive and last for years before it needs replacing.

Seed can also be sown directly outside but not before all danger of frost has passed. Double-check the manufacturer's instructions on your seed packet for regional recommendations on sowing outside. Prepare ground as above and sow seed sparsely in lines. Remember they will need thinning out and each plant can grow fairly large.

Container Growing

Oregano is an ideal container plant and will grow happily in a pot on a windowsill or any bright spot indoors.

The most important thing about growing oregano in pots or containers is making sure they are well drained. Put a layer of gravel at the bottom of the pot to ensure good drainage.

Harvesting

When growing well, a few leaves can be picked from each plant when needed. Once the plants are 20 cm. (8 in.) high, use as required—the more oregano is used, the more foliage it will produce. Flowers can be picked off as they appear to encourage more leaf growth. If you want the plants to flower, harvest plenty of leaves before they start to develop flowers.

Plants may get woody or straggly after three or four years and need replacing, although many plants in ideal conditions will last much longer. Break off dead wood in the winter or early spring before shoots appear. Plants can be cut to shape when they start getting straggly.

Oregano is a stunning plant and produces bright green foliage that looks attractive in pots on a balcony or patio, as well as being a practical hanging-basket plant. Pick oregano leaves from a hanging basket outside the kitchen door and wow the family with your culinary skills. Remember to water in dry weather.

Using and storing oregano

Oregano often stays green and usable for most of the year, dying back in late autumn or winter and returning in early spring, however, sprigs can be frozen or dried. To freeze, spread fresh sprigs or individual leaves onto a tray and freeze quickly. Put into a container or bag and label. To dry oregano, small sprigs should be hung upside down in a dry airy place in paper bags to collect broken leaves and to protect from dust. Crumble dry leaves into a labelled jar and store out of direct light.

Oregano has been used to aid digestive disorders and in preparations to help soothe coughs and sore throats in children. It is also a good antiseptic and has sedative properties. For this reason, oregano shouldn't be taken in large doses.

Parsley

Although parsley is one of the most widespread and well-know herbs, it is often underused—curly-leafed parsley is an attractive garnish that is often left on the side of a plate. Parsley is packed with vitamins and iron and is a fairly easy biennial plant to grow. It produces plenty of foliage in the first year and develops flowers and seeds during the second. Sowing parsley every year will ensure a constant supply.

Parsley has been cultivated for many centuries, and was used as a table garnish even in the ancient world. Because of its powerful healing properties and culinary uses, parsley has been considered a wonder herb. Parsley probably originated in the Mediterranean region, where it still grows wild in some areas. It is now grown commercially and domestically in many countries around the world. There are different varieties, including the well-known curly-leafed type and a flat-leafed "Italian" variety.

High C

Parsley contains more vitamin C, gram for gram, than many citrus fruits. It is useful as a vegetable crop as well as an herb, as its vitamins are easily absorbed into the body.

Growing advice

Parsley can be propagated by seed but you can also buy ready-growing plants from suppliers.

Propagation by seed

Generally parsley seed can be sown fairly early in the spring, although double-check your seed packet for variety and regional variations first. Sow seed in well-drained pots or trays of fresh compost. Parsley is a heavy-feeding plant and won't thrive if started in poor garden soil.

Parsley seeds can take up to six weeks to germinate and will need to be kept warm during that time. Compost should be watered regularly to keep it moist. Some growers soak their seeds in water overnight to speed up the germination process.

When the seedlings are large enough to handle, they should be thinned to allow growing space. Remove the weakest and leave one plant per pot. The seedlings pulled out can be replanted individually in new pots of fresh compost or added to salads. When plants are established, two or three healthy plants may be enough for an average household, although parsley can be used as a vegetable, so if you have the space, grow more than you think you will need.

Planting out

After all danger of frost has passed, plants can be put out in the garden. Choose a well-drained sunny spot, although parsley will tolerate some shade, and position one or two in the vegetable patch so you don't forget to use it. Prepare the soil by digging over and removing any perennial weeds. Parsley is a heavy feeder and will thrive in a rich soil; if possible, dig in some well-rotted manure or compost during the early spring before parsley plants go out.

Digging deeply before planting will allow the long tap root to fully develop, resulting in plenty of healthy foliage as well as a root that can be eaten. Water regularly but don't let the ground become waterlogged.

During the growing period, parsley plants will benefit from an organic feed every few weeks. This plant takes minerals and vitamins up from the soil resulting in highly nutritious leaves and roots, so a little organic food from time to time will result in the best crops.

Parsley seeds can also be sown outside. Prepare a seed bed in the spring, but seed shouldn't be sown until all danger of frost has passed. Parsley can take a while to become established and grow well, so in regions where summers aren't so reliable, sowing seed inside and putting out small plants in late spring is usually the best option. Wherever seed is sown, sow sparsely as plants will need thinning out later to allow space to develop and grow. Check your seed packet for spacing recommendations, but generally an average plant will need at least 30 cm. (12 in.) to grow into.

Ready-grown plants

Because seeds can take so long to germinate, sometimes starting your parsley patch with ready-grown plants is more practical. Buy healthy plants from a good supplier. Plants bought from garden

Container Growing

Parsley grows well in containers, but must never be allowed to dry out. Use well-drained pots of fresh compost and sow seeds sparsely or plant out with one or two ready-grown plants, depending on the size of the pot. In colder climates, a pot of parsley can be kept indoors over winter and will often produce leaves until the following spring. Try growing a couple of varieties in each pot, size permitting, and position in a sunny spot. Remember to water regularly in dry weather.

suppliers have often been grown in a warm environment and won't be used to the cold, so don't be tempted to rush home and put them directly outside. Keep indoors or in a warm greenhouse until the weather warms up and harden them off by putting out in the sun during the day and bringing in at night for a few days.

Parsley is a biennial plant; in its second year it will develop flowers and seeds and very little foliage. Seeds can be collected and resown the following year. To ensure a constant supply of fresh parsley leaves, new plants will need to be grown every year.

Parsley plants should be watered regularly in dry weather and kept weed-free to ensure the roots take up all the nutrients they can.

Using and storing parsley

Although often used as a simple garnish, parsley is a herb that should be eaten as well as looked at. Chop fresh parsley leaves finely and sprinkle over a dish to get the full benefit. An old Cornish recipe using parsley as the main ingredient was an economical family pie. Chopped parsley leaves were mixed with any leftover meat and covered or enclosed with pastry before baking.

Parsley can be frozen or dried. Freeze whole stems quickly and label the container before storing in the freezer. To dry, sprigs can be hung in paper bags in a dry airy place until crisp. Crumble into labelled jars and store out of direct light.

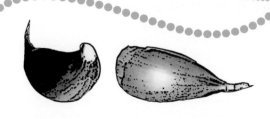

Parsley helps freshen the breath so is a great herb to grow if you happen to eat a lot of garlic in your diet!

Rosemary

Rosemary is a hardy evergreen shrub and, in the right environment, will last for up to twenty years. Cultivated for centuries, rosemary has collected a host of myths and legends—it has been used in blessings, wedding ceremonies and also to ward off evil spirits. This aromatic herb has also played an important medicinal role, and is believed to help alleviate tension, colds and other minor ailments.

Although originally from warmer Mediterranean areas, rosemary is grown in many parts of the world and gets hardier the further north it is grown. Rosemary will often stay green and fresh even when weighed down by snow.

Because of its hardiness, it is often included in herb gardens and will tolerate a certain amount of neglect. It is an attractive shrub, producing flowers once a year and plenty of foliage. Rosemary can grow quite tall, up to 1 mt. (3½ ft.) or more depending on conditions, so it should be positioned behind lower-growing plants to avoid over-shadowing.

Growing advice

Generally the best way to propagate rosemary is by cutting and sometimes by layering. As with many hardy shrubs, propagating from seed isn't always easy, although it can be done.

Propagating by seed

If you are starting rosemary from seed, it's a good idea to have a plan B in place. Seeds can take up to three months to germinate and the trays or pots will need to be kept warm and watered regularly during that time. Although rosemary will sometimes tolerate near-drought conditions, in the early stages of growth, seeds and seedlings will need regular watering.

Sow seeds in well-drained trays or pots of fresh compost and follow the particular recommendations on the seed packet. Generally seed should be started in early spring. Keep in a warm greenhouse or indoors in a bright spot until the plants are large enough to be repotted into containers or planted outside.

Rosemary plants grow into fairly large shrubs and, unless they are to be used as a decorative feature in the garden, one or two fully grown plants may be sufficient for an average family's use. However, due to the poor germination rate, sow the whole packet of seeds and adhere to any growing tips provided by the seed manufacturer.

When seedlings are growing well, and after all danger of a frost has passed, rosemary plants can be repotted into containers outside or planted out into the garden. Allow 45 cm. (8 in.) or more between plants if planted in rows, or use as border plants and put one or two in the herb bed. When positioning in the garden, avoid draughty or windy spots. Although rosemary is a hardy shrub and will tolerate cold winters, it doesn't appreciate strong cold winds combined with heavy rainfall and low temperatures.

Propagation from cuttings Choose a healthy well-established plant from which to take cuttings, and wait until the plant has finished flowering. Two or three plants are usually ample for an average family, but take more cuttings than needed, as not all will develop roots.

Cut 8–10 cm. (3–4 in.) pieces of healthy stems, just above or below a leaf joint, and push these cuttings into a well-drained pot of fresh compost. Keep pots in a warm place and cover with plastic, or use a propagator if available. Established rosemary plants will tolerate near-drought conditions, but while the cuttings are developing roots they will need water from time to time. Don't allow the pots to become waterlogged though. Cuttings should take around two months to develop roots.

Planting on

After all danger of frost has passed, plant out in the herb garden or into large pots or containers. Cuttings can be started in a well-prepared seed bed, but in colder regions, they will need protection during the winter months.

Use rosemary sprigs as soon as the plants are growing well. Cut whole sprigs and remove leaves or add whole sprigs to the roasting tin.

Growing Tip

Rosemary is fairly tolerant of poor soils but doesn't thrive particularly well in acidic soil. Add lime to your soil if it is very acidic before planting out rosemary plants.

Container Growing

Rosemary grows well in containers and doesn't mind drying out occasionally, although to keep your plants fresh and green, water regularly, especially in hot sunny periods. Always use well-drained pots or containers and fill with non-acidic soil or preferably fresh compost.

Shrubs can grow fairly large so adequate-sized pots will ensure the plants grow well. Rosemary flowers every year and stays green throughout the year so makes an attractive patio or balcony plant. Choose a sunny spot out of cold draughts.

Using and storing rosemary

Rosemary has always been considered an important medicinal herb with good reason. Its natural properties can help alleviate stress-related conditions such as headaches and nervous tension. Put a few leaves or sprigs of rosemary in a muslin bag and allow water to run through it while filling a bath. Relax and ease away tension.

Rosemary oil is used externally for insect bites and is used extensively in the cosmetic industry. However, because rosemary oil is quite a strong essential oil, it is not advisable to use it neat because of this strength; dilute in a safe carrier oil first.

The leaves and sprigs add a touch of magic to a roast dinner. Whole sprigs of rosemary or just the leaves can be added to a roasting tin during cooking, so that the natural flavors of the herb seep into the food. Strip leaves and use the stems as skewers to cook meat and vegetables on the barbecue or add whole sprigs to the embers of a fire to perfume the air and deter mosquitoes.

Rosemary doesn't usually need storing, as it will stay green through the winter. However, it can be dried if a very cold winter is expected. Hang sprigs upside down in paper bags until the needles fall. Store in airtight labelled jars out of direct light. Drying can reduce the flavor.

Sage

A hardy perennial woody shrub native to the Mediterranean regions, sage grows well in cooler climates and can live for many years in an established position in a herb garden. Plants can get straggly after a few years, and many growers will advise replanting every five years.

Sage has been used medicinally and in the kitchen for thousands of years and was believed to bestow wisdom, hence the common name. Ancient people considered it to be the herb of good health and psychic powers, and, in Roman times, sage was known as the herb of immortality. Sage is a pungent herb that was grown to mask the smells from open sewers in urban areas during medieval times.

Although sage is now grown chiefly as a culinary herb, and has a starring role in sage and onion stuffing recipes, it is still used in alternative medicinal therapies and by herbalists.

Once established, sage is an easy herb to maintain, needing very little attention. Variegated varieties are now available and it is possible to make a very attractive display of sages, particularly when they flower.

Growing advice

There are a number of ways to propagate sage—plants can be started from seed, by layering or taking cuttings. Growing from seed is very satisfying, but the plants will need a year to become established before they can be used. Layering is the most commonly used method but cuttings are also quite successful.

Propagation by seed

Although sage will need to be growing for a year before it can be used, if you start your plants using seed it does allow more choice of variety. Variegated types producing different colored leaves and flowers are available from good garden suppliers and will enhance a patio or herb garden; like all sages they will need very little looking after once they are well-established.

Check on the seed packet for growing recommendations, but generally sage seed should be sown in early spring. Sow in well-drained pots or trays of fresh compost. Water regularly to keep compost damp but not wet. Keep trays and pots indoors or in a warm greenhouse until all danger of frost has passed, at which time plants can be put outside in containers or directly into the garden.

Sage will thrive in part-sun/part-shade and, as it is fairly tolerant of near-drought conditions, sage will grow well on a rockery or in a walled garden. Good drainage is essential.

Planting on

Dig over the soil fairly deeply. The deeper the soil is dug, the deeper the roots of your plants will travel to find water. Remove any perennial weeds, large stones and non-organic debris buried in the soil.

Plants can grow quite large, so allow enough room for them to grow into. Follow the recommendation on your seed packet if growing from seed, but generally about 60 cm. (2 ft.) should be allowed for each plant. Plant outside as soon as all danger of frost has passed. Although sage is a hardy perennial and will survive very cold winters, young plants will need warmth to help them develop roots and become established. Water immediately after planting and keep weed-free and watered regularly, especially in dry weather until plants are growing well.

Plants grown from seed should be allowed to grow for a year before leaves are picked.

Propagation from cuttings

In early spring or summer, preferably before flowering, take 8–10 cm. (3–4 in.) cuttings from branches of a well-established healthy plant. Push cut ends of cuttings into a well-drained pot or container of fresh compost. Keep the container out of draughts in a fairly sheltered place. Water regularly until the cuttings have developed roots. This may be the following autumn or sometimes not until the following spring. Allow more cuttings than you need as not all of them may take. Plant out as soon as the plants are growing well, in a prepared spot in the garden or in large containers.

Propagation by layering

This is probably the easiest and most successful way to propagate sage plants. Choose a well-established plant and find a low-growing healthy branch. Lay this out across the soil next to your plant, and mark where it naturally touches the ground.

Container Growing

Although a hardy plant, sage doesn't like long, cold, wet winters, so if grown in containers, it can be brought indoors in the winter months. Sage thrives in a container as long as it is well-drained and large enough. Plants can get very woody after a few years and should be replaced if necessary, although a healthy sage plant in an ideal spot can last for many years.

Sage is an attractive container plant for a patio or balcony, and the new variegated types create an attractive display. The soil shouldn't be allowed to dry out completely but never over-water sage.

Prepare this area of soil well, taking care not to damage roots of the established plant. Lay the lower branch over the prepared soil and peg down with a wooden or plastic U-shaped peg. Use whatever is available but make sure there aren't any sharp points on the peg that could damage the branch.

Cover the pegged part of the branch with 2 cm. (1 in.) or so of soil and water carefully. Within a season or two, the branch will have produced roots and can be cut from the mother plant. The new plant can be replanted or left if there is enough space for it to grow.

After flowering, sage plants can become straggly. Prune back to the shape you want, and above all, keep using it in the kitchen.

Using and storing sage

Sage has volatile oils that contain toxins, and so should never be taken in large doses. It has been used in medicinal preparations for centuries and is widely used today to treat some menopausal symptoms.

It is a strong-tasting herb and should be used sparingly in cooking as it can drown other flavors. Sage and onion stuffing is perhaps one of the most widely known recipes, and although it can be bought ready-made or dried, making your own with fresh sage is a great alternative.

Sage can be frozen, although in milder climates, plants may stay green throughout the year. Freeze individual leaves quickly, put into a bag or container and label before storing in the freezer. Stems can be hung and dried in paper bags, in an airy place indoors. When completely dry, crumble into labelled jars. Store out of direct light.

Thyme

A hardy perennial shrub that will live for many years in the garden before it needs to be replaced, thyme has long been cultivated for culinary and medicinal purposes. Thyme was used for many generations to help preserve meat. Its flavors release slowly and should be added early in the cooking time of most recipes. It is also a useful medicinal herb and will help alleviate cold symptoms.

A number of varieties can be grown, however, *Thymus vulgaris* and *Thymus* x *citriodorus* (lemon-scented) are two that tend to be stronger in flavor and scent than newer hybrid varieties. Thyme is native to the Mediterranean regions and will tolerate a fairly dry climate. In wetter climates, it needs to be in a very well-drained spot; it is also an ideal container or rockery herb.

Thyme Myths

Myths and legends have attached themselves to this herb over the centuries—one belief was that a sprig of thyme worn in a woman's hair would attract a husband.

Growing advice

Thyme can be propagated from seed although it will be a year before the plants are ready to use. Growing your own plants from seed is very satisfying if you are prepared to wait. Being a woody shrub, thyme is more often propagated by root division or from cuttings.

Propagation by seed
Check on your seed packet for regional variations, but generally thyme seed can be started in early spring as long as the seed trays are kept warm and watered regularly. Fill well-drained pots or trays with fresh compost and sow seeds. Keep warm and watered. Compost should never be too wet, but at this stage, trays or pots shouldn't be allowed to dry out completely. When plants are large enough to handle and all danger of frost has passed, plants can be put out into the garden.

Planting on
Choose a sunny well-drained spot and prepare the soil by digging over and removing any perennial weeds. Large stones are not necessarily a problem for thyme as it will also thrive in rockeries, on stone walls and in hanging baskets and other containers.

Once the plants are in position, water regularly. Don't let the soil get too wet or dry out completely. Thyme will be happier in a rockery rather than a vegetable plot in wetter climates. It is perennial so a permanent place is desirable.

Seeds can also be sown directly outside later on in the spring, after all danger of frost has passed. Sow seeds in drills about 30 cm. (12 in.) apart, in very well prepared soil, raked to a fine consistency—a seed bed is ideal. Sow quite sparsely as plants will need to be thinned out later to allow growing room. Check any manufacturer's growing recommendations on your seed packet. As long as the soil is well drained, thyme can be a useful groundcover plant in spots around the garden.

When seedlings are overcrowded, pull out every other plant or so. If pulled up carefully, the seedlings can be replanted. Allow at least 30 cm. (12 in.) for plants to grow into. A well-established thyme shrub in ideal conditions will spread over a fairly large area, and one or two plants may be enough for a family's requirements.

Propagation by root division

After three or four years plants can become straggly, which is an ideal time to propagate by root division. In late summer or early spring and using only healthy well-established plants, gently loosen the soil with a fork around the plant and dig up carefully, limiting root damage as much as possible.

Firmly but gently pull roots apart into two or more clumps and replant immediately. A thyme plant in a pot makes an attractive gift and will stay green through most of the winter if kept warm and in a bright spot.

Propagation by cuttings

Cuttings should be taken in the spring before flowering from a healthy established plant. Cut 8–10 cm. (2–4 in.) pieces from fresh stems and push cut ends into well-drained pots

Container Growing

Such an attractive plant deserves its own special place in the garden and will thrive in a well-drained container or large pot on a patio or balcony. Thyme will also grow on a kitchen windowsill given enough sunlight and water.

Although this herb will tolerate near-drought conditions, when growing in pots, it should be watered from time to time especially in dry weather periods or if grown indoors.

Repot every two or three years and treat to an organic feed from time to time. If a very cold winter is expected, plants can be brought inside or a mulch applied to protect the roots during the winter months.

of fresh compost or directly outside in a well-prepared seed bed. Outside cuttings may need protection during the first winter while they are still developing roots. Water regularly—at this stage, plants shouldn't be allowed to dry out, but must be growing in well-drained soil or compost.

When cuttings have produced roots in the autumn or following spring, they can be repotted or planted out in the herb garden. Thyme will tolerate fairly cold temperatures, but if a very cold winter is expected, a mulch or plastic cover will help protect the roots. Remove any protection early in the spring.

Thyme is an attractive ground-cover plant and will flower every year. When bruised or brushed against, the leaves release an intoxicating scent.

Using and storing thyme

Thyme is a practical family herb and has long been used to alleviate symptoms of the common cold. Simply steep leaves in boiling water for five minutes, strain, and sip when cool enough. A spoonful of honey or a dash of lemon adds flavor and nutrients.

Thyme is a natural antiseptic and is a good quick cure for minor cuts and grazes. Simply rub leaves onto and around the affected part.

Thyme leaves are often available all year round, but it can be stored successfully. Dry sprigs upside down in paper bags in a dry airy place in the house. Or lay on trays in a sunny spot until leaves are crisp and dry. Crumble and store in labelled glass jars out of direct light.

Stems can also be frozen. Pick stems as flowers are starting to appear, lay on trays and freeze quickly.

Watercress

Native to Europe and Asia and now growing over many parts of the world, watercress has been considered a superfood for many years and has been used as a medicinal herb for many centuries. Watercress became a commercial crop in the nineteenth century. By the early twentieth century it had become a very important herb and, at one point, London was at the heart of the world's watercress industry.

Nutritional Powerhouse

Used for many years to encourage growth in children and strengthen soldiers before battle, the health benefits of this herb are stunning. Watercress has more vitamin C, gram for gram, than citrus fruit, plenty of potassium, iron, and significant quantities of calcium. Because of these amazing qualities, watercress is a good immune-booster, helping to protect and strengthen our immune systems.

Watercress is often found growing wild in streams. However, if there are grazing animals or chemicals being used on land nearby, the roots of watercress plants can take up toxins, making it unwise to eat. It can also be infested with liver flukes. The taste isn't always affected, but the properties of the plant will be. To be sure of a clean supply, try growing your own rather than collecting it from the wild.

Land cress is a good substitute if running water is a problem. Although it will need watering regularly, land cress can be grown in a herb or vegetable patch and will stay green for much of the year. The plant is vitamin-rich but has slightly less flavor than traditional watercress.

Growing advice

For many years it was assumed that watercress could only be grown in a stream of running water. But with a little forward planning, it can be grown at home. Some growers use a children's paddling pool but watercress can be grown almost anywhere as long as it has sufficient clean water—roots will rot in stagnant water as they will for most plants.

Propagation by seed
Buy seeds from a good supplier and check any growing recommendations for your region. Land cress is the better option if you are intending to grow cress in the vegetable patch, as watercress does need plenty of water, which may be too much for most vegetable crops.

Start seeds in well-drained pots or trays of fresh compost. Compost must be kept wet but shouldn't hold water as it will stagnate. Seeds won't germinate in dry compost or stagnant water. As long as the pots are well drained and watered often the seeds should germinate well.

Plant out when seedlings are large enough to handle and all danger of frost has passed. Watercress isn't a sun-loving plant and will thrive in partial shade.

A garden pond can be used to grow watercress. However, it must be cleaned regularly and have a constant water supply gently pumped through. The most important thing is not to let the water become stagnant or polluted.

Watercress isn't a true water plant as it grows above the water level so a location closely resembling a shallow stream is ideal. Plants will also grow successfully on the bank of a stream. With the right water conditions, watercress will grow through many months of the year and can be harvested as required.

An old paddling pool is a useful container for watercress. Make sure it is very well drained and fill with fresh compost or fairly rich soil, sieved if necessary. Plant seedlings or young plants and water immediately after planting. Once established, watercress can become an invasive plant, although not usually so prolific as mint. Because of the conditions watercress requires to thrive, it's generally easy to contain the plants and prevent them from taking over.

Warning

Always ensure that animal droppings and chemicals haven't seeped into the soil or water supply as watercress takes up toxins undetectable through taste, which are dangerous to consume. Also be on the lookout for liver flukes if gathering watercress from the wild.

Container Growing

Watercress should be contained although not necessarily in the usual way with ceramic pots and decorative troughs. Plants are best grown in ponds, streams, and paddling pools and, as mentioned above, need a constant water supply or to be watered regularly.

They also need good drainage if planted in compost or soil. Poorly growing plants are usually suffering from waterlogging in stagnant water.

Propagation from cuttings

Watercress can be started from cuttings from a shop-bought bunch of healthy stems, preferably organic. Put a few stems into a glass or small vase of water and change the water daily until roots develop. Plant out in the garden or pond as soon as possible or when the nights aren't too cold. In milder regions, watercress may be available right throughout the year, although winter watercress tends to be slightly coarser.

Using and storing watercress

In the right environment watercress will be available all year round. Keep one or two stems in a glass of water to develop new roots and shoots. The water must be changed daily. Fresh stems can also be kept in the salad compartment of the fridge for a couple of days.

Because of its incredible nutritional qualities, a daily portion of watercress will help boost the immune system and provide resistance to colds and flu. Add to salads in the summer months. Chopped leaves and stems can be added to stir-frys in the spring and summer, and to casseroles and stews in the winter. It also makes a wonderful summer soup. Watercress is a useful edible garnish.

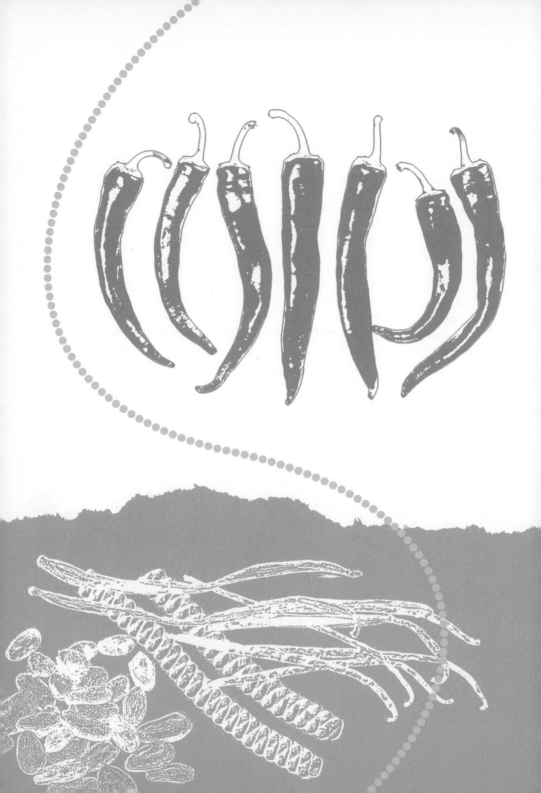

Spices

The ancient spice trade, in which herbs, drugs and spices were caravanned or shipped around the world, was filled with romance and mystery. The origins of some spices were kept secret, allowing traders to charge extraordinary prices for these much sought-after products. Today, however, we have the information necessary to grow these wonderful plants at home. Knowing where the plants originate is crucial to getting their growing conditions right.

Home-grown spices

Spices are often thought of as plants that can only be grown in hot or tropical climates, and for many that's true, but there a fair few spices that can be grown in a moderate climate, given a little TLC. Some will naturally grow in cooler climates while others prefer a tropical environment.

Spices are classified as the roots, seeds, stigmas (sometimes called fronds), and bark of plant, whereas herbs are generally considered to be the leafy part of the plant. In this section the spices we cover are caraway (seeds), chili peppers (pods and seeds), fenugreek (seeds), garlic (bulbs/seeds), ginger (root), horseradish (root), mustard (seeds), poppies (seeds), and saffron (stigmas). Some plants have multiple uses. A selection of plants producing both herbs and spices can be found in "One Plant, Several Uses" (see pages 16–33).

Caraway

An underrated spice, caraway is generally grown only for the seed, however its roots are said to be as tasty as many root vegetables. Caraway has grown wild across Europe and Asia for thousands of years, and has been used as a culinary and medicinal herb for centuries. For our purposes we can treat caraway as a spice, but the leaves can be used as well as the roots and seeds. Although it is a little invasive, caraway is a wonderful plant to include in a herb garden and is easy to grow.

Growing advice

Because caraway plants have tap roots, they don't transplant easily so the seed should be sown *in situ* in a sunny well-drained spot. Prepare the ground well.

Caraway will thrive in lighter soils—heavy clays tend to stunt the growth of their roots. Dig over fairly deeply, especially if you want to harvest good healthy roots as well as the leaves and seeds of the plant. Incorporate sand to lighten the soil if necessary. Remove all perennial weeds and large stones and rake the soil over to a fine consistency.

Propagation by seed
Seeds can be sown in spring and summer, and usually have a successful germination rate. Double-check the manufacturer's recommended sowing times on your seed packet before you start.

Seeds sown in spring will flower the following year and autumn-sown seeds will flower the following summer. Autumn-sown seeds should be protected in cold winters with a cloche or other similar cover. Protect seedlings and small plants until temperatures warm up. Larger, more established plants may survive with a layer of mulch around the base of each plant. Don't mulch too closely as the stem needs air circulation.

Fresh seed tends to germinate more readily than seed that has been kept for a while. Sow thinly along a row or around the garden, but thin out later as they become overcrowded. The small plants you remove can be used in the kitchen. Allow about 20 cm. (8 in.) of space for each plant to grow into. Caraway plants grow to around 30 cm. (12 in.) high.

Growing on
Pick leaves regularly during the first year of growth to encourage more root development. From time to time, hoe gently around the plants to remove any weeds or weed by hand. Generally, caraway is a hardy plant but can sometimes be attacked by caterpillars. Growing other strong-scented herbs close by can often deter insects. A garlic plant in each row of seeds may help.

In the second year of growth when the flowers start to dry, remove them from the plant. If left to self-seed, caraway can become invasive in the herb garden, although unless protected against the winter in cold climates, seed may not germinate.

Container Growing

Caraway can become invasive in the garden in milder climates, and therefore makes an ideal candidate for container growing. However, because of the long tap root, the containers will need to be very deep and well draining. If these conditions are met, then caraway should grow very happily in a container.

Barrel-shaped containers full of caraway with their feathery, very decorative foliage make attractive patio planters.

Using and storing caraway

Seeds

Caraway seeds can be collected by removing the flower heads from the plant when they start to dry and then hanging them upside down in paper bags. The seeds should be stored in a labelled glass jar out of direct light. Light will reduce the flavor. Generally, the leaves aren't stored, but could be dried and stored in the same way as the seeds. Caraway seeds are traditionally added to seed cake, a tea loaf cake much loved by the Victorians. They are also commonly used in Eastern European breads.

Roots

Caraway roots can be harvested and kept for a day or two in the fridge before eating. Like parsnips, caraway root is sweeter after a frost, but if harvested before the frosts arrive, keeping it in the fridge for a couple of days will sweeten the taste.

Chili peppers

Although chili peppers are native to warmer climes, they grow remarkably well in cooler regions. They are in the same family—*Capsicum*—as sweet peppers and need more or less the same growing conditions.

Nutritional Notes

Chili peppers have been cultivated for thousands of years. They are not only a very popular spicy addition to food, but also high in nutritional value. With significant amounts of C, A and B vitamins, chilis are also a good source of potassium and iron. The high vitamin C content make chilis a practical addition to beans, pulses, and foods somewhat lower in vitamin C .

Chilis are also believed to ward off evil in some cultures and are hung, along with a lemon, over a doorway into the house.

Growing advice

Generally, chili peppers should be treated as you would sweet peppers, although they can be less tolerant of cold weather so check on the manufacturer's recommended sowing times on your seed packet for your particular region before you start.

Propagation by seed

Start seed in well-drained trays or pots of fresh potting or seed compost. Keep warm and watered until seedlings appear and are large enough to handle. When they have three or four true leaves, repot into individual pots or plant out in the herb bed or vegetable patch. Make sure all danger of frost has passed and the soil and air temperatures have warmed up. Although they may tolerate some cold, a frost or huge temperature drop could kill very young plants.

Planting on

Dig over the soil in a sunny well-drained spot, remove any weeds and large stones and rake or hoe to a fairly fine consistency. Dip the pots in water before you remove the plants to limit root damage and gently but firmly plant out in rows or around the garden. Allow at least 45 cm. (18 in.) of space for each plant to grow into. Chili plants can help deter bugs from vegetable crops.

Keep plants weed-free and make sure they get enough water in dry periods. Chili peppers will thrive in a sunny spot in the garden. However, if the leaves start wilting, they may be getting too much sun. Provide shade during the hottest part of the day but remember to remove the shade later.

Use chili peppers as and when they become available. Check on the seed packet for maturity patterns. They can often be eaten green or left until red. In cooler climates, sweet peppers don't always reach the "red" stage, but chili peppers are smaller and ripen more quickly than larger peppers.

Container Growing

Chili pepper plants are attractive and ideally suited to container growing. Fill well-drained pots with fresh compost and plant seedlings or young plants firmly, taking care to handle stems and roots as little as possible. Water well after planting.

Keep a plant or two in a large pot or container in a sunny spot in the house, or on a patio or balcony. Chilis are also a great plant to grow in a greenhouse as they can deter bugs from your other greenhouse crops. Keep out of cold draughts and remember to water them.

Using and storing chilis

Chilis can be used fresh but they are often dried. Leave to ripen on the plant and remove in dry weather. Leave in a dark airy place until dried completely and then store in labelled glass jars. Keep jars out of direct light to avoid loss of flavor and color. Peppers can also be strung up like mushrooms over a warm range or radiator, although care should be taken that they don't collect dust.

Use chili peppers in all recipes that demand a spicy taste. The obvious choice would be to add some to a chili con carne dish. Chop finely before using. Avoid using seeds if you prefer a milder taste. Always wash your hands thoroughly after handling chili peppers, especially the seeds, which are the hottest part of the pepper. Don't touch your eyes or mouth before washing your hands.

Fenugreek

Native to Asia and the Mediterranean, fenugreek has grown wild and in cultivation over most of the world for centuries. Fenugreek is best known for its spicy seed, used in many different dishes, especially in Indian food. The seeds can be used fresh or roasted, as a coffee substitute or a powdered spice. Sprouting seeds can also be eaten—add them to salads. The seed also provides a useful yellow dye.

Leaves from the fenugreek plant are also edible and can be added to curry dishes. Fenugreek is employed as a fodder crop and has in the past been used in many medicinal preparations. It is now mostly used in Ayurvedic and other alternative therapy medications.

Growing advice

In tropical climates fenugreek plants will complete their growth cycle in as little as sixteen weeks; however, in cooler climates this may take about four weeks longer. The plant prefers a warmer climate so growing in a warm greenhouse or conservatory may be advisable if you live in a cooler region.

Buy your seed from a reputable company and check on the manufacturer's growing recommendations before you start. Growers recommend soaking the seed in water for about twelve hours before sowing.

Propagation by seed

Sow seed *in situ* in the spring, or as soon as the temperature has risen significantly after the winter. Choose a sunny spot in the garden and dig over the ground removing large stones and perennial weeds. Hoe or rake to a fine consistency. Make sure the area is well drained, as roots will rot quickly in waterlogged soil. Keep weed-free and watered in very dry weather. Seeds normally germinate in a couple of days.

Growing on

Plants should be thinned to allow at least 15. cm (5–6 in.) of growing room per plant, and, as fenugreek enjoys fertile soil, an organic feed or added compost will help your plants thrive. In cooler climates, sow fenugreek seed in a greenhouse and make sure the soil doesn't dry out. The more tropical environment you can create for your plants, the better.

When the pods have ripened on the plants, remove and let them dry out in the sun or in a bright spot indoors for a few hours. When the plants have died back completely, cut the plant down at ground level leaving the roots in the ground. Fenugreek roots contain useful nitrogen for the soil and will benefit your crops next season.

Sprouting Seeds

Fenugreek seed can be "sprouted" like many other plant seeds in a glass or plastic tumbler. Pour a thin layer of seeds into the tumbler and add tepid water over the seeds, swishing them around for a few seconds to soak thoroughly. Cover the jar with a piece of muslin and secure with an elastic band. Drain all the water through the muslin, then keep the jar in a warm dark cupboard.

Repeat the watering process in the morning and evening, and seeds should start to sprout in two or three days. Eat when they are 2 cm. (1 in.) long.

Container Growing

Large, fairly deep pots or containers should be used for fenugreek. Make sure they are well drained and fill with fresh organic compost. Feed plants regularly during the growing season. Pots and containers are good to use in cooler climates as they can be moved to catch the sunniest spots or brought indoors when the nights get too cold.

Don't let compost dry out but never over-water; creating a near-tropical environment will encourage your plants to thrive.

Using and storing fenugreek

After removing ripe pods from the plants, lay these in the sun for a few hours to dry out, or spread in a bright spot indoors. Then either store the whole pods in labelled jars and keep out of direct light, or remove the seeds first and store in the same way. Seeds must be completely dry before storing.

Fenugreek can be used in many recipes and is a useful medicinal herb. Dried seeds can be used fresh or roasted first. They are strong in taste so should be used in moderation. Add to homemade stews, curries, soups, and breads. Roasted fenugreek seeds can be used as a coffee substitute. Seeds can also be sprouted and added to salads.

Garlic

Grown in the wild for thousands of years, there is evidence of garlic being cultivated 3000 years ago. A member of the onion (*Allium*) family, garlic will tolerate cool temperatures, although the plants may not survive a heavy frost.

Growing advice

Garlic can be started using an organic bulb bought from a supermarket, however, hybrids grown especially for cultivation will probably have a higher success rate.

Vampire Deterrent

Garlic has always been considered an important herb/spice and has gathered around it many myths and legends, including the one about keeping vampires away. Today it is used in many health and medicinal preparations because of its anti-fungal and antibiotic qualities.

It is widely believed that garlic can help prevent colds and flu, and on top of all that, it is a must-have in an active kitchen. Grow parsley in your herb garden to help freshen the breath after eating garlic.

Container Growing

Plant cloves in a well-drained, fairly deep container full of fresh compost. The soil in pots and containers can dry out quickly, especially in a sunny spot, so water regularly, but don't allow pots to become waterlogged.

Plant a clove or two in large pots already containing other crops. The garlic will help deter pests. Allow about 20 cm. (8 in.) of space for each bulb to develop, then treat as you would if they were in the vegetable patch.

Propagation by cloves

Garlic cloves can usually be planted fairly early in the year, but the ground has to be workable. Prepare a sunny, well-drained part of the garden; dig over the soil and remove any perennial weeds and large stones. Hoe or rake to a fine consistency and push your garlic cloves into the soil at 20 cm. (8 in.) intervals along a row. Or they can be planted here and there around the vegetable patch if the soil has been prepared. Garlic can help deter pests from your crops.

Leave the tip of each clove just slightly above the level of the soil. If you have a problem with birds, sprinkle a little soil over the tip of each clove. Or use a wildlife-friendly netting to protect the cloves until they start to to produce shoots.

Water after planting, then keep weed-free and watered in dry periods. Generally, garlic doesn't need much watering early in the season, but never let it dry out later in the summer months.

Growing on

If your plants start to bolt or run to seed, either bend the offending flower stem down and hopefully, it will decide to put its energy back into the bulb. Often, the bulb won't develop any more but it can still be used in the kitchen. Use straight away as these runaway bulbs don't tend to store well.

When the leaves start dying back, make sure they are protected from too much rain. Then, when they have died back completely, fork carefully around each bulb to loosen the soil then pull the bulbs up and lay them in the sun for a couple of hours to dry. Turn them over every so often.

The strong smell of garlic deters pests and its natural anti-bacterial properties protect it from diseases. It's unusual for garlic plants to suffer with viruses or bug attacks. If plants aren't doing well, it's usually because they are lacking light or water.

Depending on when they were planted, cloves should develop into full-sized bulbs between summer and autumn.

Using and storing garlic

After digging up, lay the garlic bulbs on racks or cardboard to finish drying and then plait them in strings of 12–14 bulbs or lay them in cardboard trays and store out of direct light. Hang plaits up in a dark, airy place, apart from the one you hang in the kitchen, of course. Garlic will store well for many months in the right environment.

Because garlic is so effective at preventing colds and other infectious conditions, it is a great spice to add to our everyday diet. It can be used in salads and salad dressings, in casseroles and soups; in stir-frys and Indian cooking. Mixed with butter and a little chopped parsley, it can turn a plain loaf into savory garlic bread.

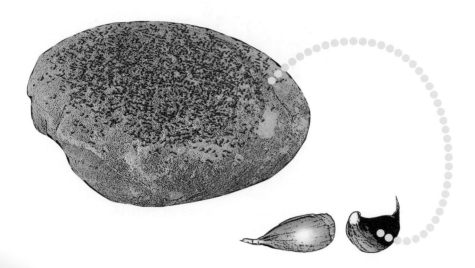

Ginger

Ginger is generally bought as a root but in fact is a rhizome (a swelling of the underground stem). Grown in Asia since ancient times, ginger has been an important commercial crop for many centuries. It has always been used to flavor food as well as being a useful medicinal plant. In recent years, science has found that ginger has properties that aid digestion, travel sickness, and various other minor ailments. So along with its culinary delights, ginger is a spice well worth growing at home for its medicinal properties.

Growing advice

Ginger is indigenous to tropical regions but will grow successfully in cooler climates, although it's unlikely you'll get a huge harvest in cooler regions. It needs warmth and is best grown under glass or plastic. As far as possible, imitate tropical conditions and your plants will thrive—keep them moist and warm with as much humidity as possible.

You can grow a ginger plant from a piece of root (rhizome) bought from a supermarket or grocer, although make sure it hasn't been treated or coated with any preservatives. Choose a piece with "eyes" that will eventually produce shoots. Sometimes these will be slightly raised from the rhizome and may even already have a shoot or two. Plant the piece of rhizome with the new shoot or eye facing upwards in a fairly large pot of rich fresh

Container Growing

If your region isn't tropical or subtropical, you will need to plant ginger in containers so it can be brought indoors during cold weather. As it rarely gets hot enough in temperate climates for ginger plants to be grown outdoors, plants should be grown indoors all year round.

Well-drained pots or containers should be about 35 cm. (14 in.) in diameter to allow space for the rhizomes to develop. Such a pot will probably be large enough for two or three plants, depending on their size. Square or oblong containers are more suitable if you intend to grow any more than two or three.

potting compost. The pot must be well drained, since ginger will rot in waterlogged soil. Pots must be regularly watered though and not allowed to dry out.

In cooler climates, ginger should be grown indoors, or in a heated greenhouse, although never in direct sun. To help the plants get going, wrap the whole pot in clear plastic after watering, and keep in a warm place until shoots begin to emerge.

In a warmer climate, ginger can be planted directly outside, although direct sun should be avoided. The plants should never be allowed to dry out and must be watered regularly in dry weather. Mulching fairly thickly around your plants will help keep moisture and nutrients in the soil.

Heavy rainfall or over-watering could wash the nutrients out of the soil, in which case an organic feed will help your plants thrive.

When the leaves die back, ginger is ready to harvest. Fork around the plants carefully to loosen the soil before digging up. Replant parts of the rhizomes you harvest and you will be getting next year's crop growing straight away.

Using and storing ginger

Ginger can be used in many culinary preparations; it is especially good added to fruit jams or orange marmalade for extra flavor. Ginger is often preserved or candied in order to store it. Ground ginger and slices of ginger root are used in many spicy recipes, and can add a touch of spice and warmth to all sorts of soups and casseroles. Both Chinese and Indian cuisines use ginger root extensively—a stir-fry or a curry would be incomplete without this useful root.

The rhizome can be used fresh and can be stored in the salad compartment of the fridge for a few days. It can also be peeled and frozen for a few months. Chop or break into pieces before freezing for convenience. Remember to label bag or freezer container.

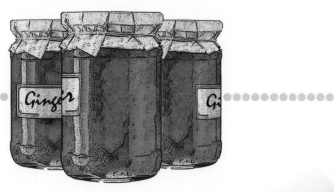

Horseradish

A perennial plant, horseradish has been used for thousands of years. The ancient Greeks used it as a liniment and it was believed to have aphrodisiac properties. During some periods, horseradish was  considered to be worth its weight in gold as a medicinal plant and has been used to treat everything from rheumatism to lung disease.

It is a prolifically growing plant, and, once established, can be difficult to contain. Because of its growing power and medicinal qualities, horseradish has been produced commercially for many years in many parts of the world. The horseradish root is spicy in taste and has significant amounts of vitamin C, calcium, and iron.

Growing advice

Horseradish can be propagated from seed or by root cuttings.

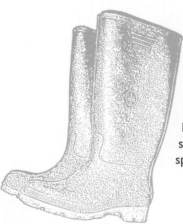

Propagation by seed

Buy seed from a good supplier and sow it in well-drained pots or trays of fresh organic compost or directly outside after all danger of frost has passed. Check on the seed packet for the growing recommendations in your region. If you are sowing seed directly outside, make sure the ground is well drained and rich, and choose a fairly sunny spot. Dig in some well-rotted manure or compost in the season prior to sowing to allow the nutrients to spread through the soil.

Dig deeply and remove large stones and perennial weeds and any non-organic debris from the soil. Root crops need a clean deep soil to develop fully. Horseradish is a fairly heavy-feeding plant, so if your soil is poor, feed it with an organic fertilizer every few weeks during the growing season.

Keep trays or outdoor lines of seeds weed-free and watered. When the seedlings are a few inches high, thin out the weaker plants to allow space for root development, or plant outside in prepared ground if you are starting them off early in trays. Allow about 30 cm. (12 in.) per plant.

Container Growing

If you have limited space for growing your herbs, spices, and vegetable crops, growing horseradish in containers may be more practical. Horseradish roots tend to be invasive if left to their own devices, and it's easy to miss one or two when digging up in the autumn.

Use deep containers; as with all root crops, horseradish needs a good depth of soil. Always use fresh compost every year to ensure the soil is full of the nutrients required to develop the roots of your plants. Don't let them dry out, but always make sure the containers are well drained as horseradish won't tolerate being waterlogged.

Propagation from root cuttings

The easiest and most common way to propagate horseradish is by root cuttings. In the autumn, dig up all the roots by forking gently around each plant, then lift the roots out carefully to minimize damage. Keep the largest roots for use in the kitchen and replant the others. Replant only the undamaged and healthy-looking roots as soon as possible after digging up. Water after planting.

Horseradish root can often be found in good garden suppliers. Check the manufacturer's growing recommendations before planting. Larger roots should be planted more deeply than smaller roots. Once established, you can keep a horseradish patch going for many years.

Using and storing horseradish

The young leaves of horseradish plants can be used in salads or chopped finely for sandwiches. Take a few leaves from each plant and never strip one plant completely of leaves.

Horseradish root will store for about a week if kept in a paper bag in the salad compartment of the fridge. Smaller roots can be stored in sand, if required, to plant the following spring, and may be edible for a few weeks. The best way to store horseradish is to make a horseradish sauce and keep in jars. Label and store out of direct light.

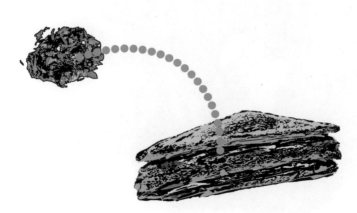

Mustard

Although mustard is a very hot-tasting spice, it doesn't need a hot climate in order to grow. Acres of mustard have been grown commercially in Europe for a very long time—certainly since the sixteenth century. English and French mustard are sold all over the world in slightly different recipe forms. In the early eighteenth century it was discovered that adding water to the fine crushed and powdered seeds of mustard produced the very hot flavor associated with English mustard. However, if the ground mustard seed is mixed with milk or cream you get a milder taste. Some French mustards have whole grains left in and, with various other ingredients, create a totally different taste to the traditionally hot English mustard.

Mustard leaves are edible and can be used as a vegetable, adding flavor to many dishes, but as the seed is generally considered to have the true mustard taste, mustard is nearly always thought of as a spice. Over the years, many countries have developed their own mustard recipes and each will have their own distinguishing flavors, consistencies and even colors.

Growing advice

Mustard grows very successfully in temperate regions because it prefers a cooler climate. Seed can be sown fairly early in the spring in most regions. White mustard is an easy crop to grow and will come up on its own year after year in an ideal environment.

Propagation by seed

Seed should be sown directly outside in a well-drained sunny spot. Prepare the soil by digging over and removing any perennial weeds and large stones, then hoe or rake over to a fine consistency. The finer the topsoil, the easier the seeds will germinate and put down roots.

Sow in rows about 0.5–1 cm. (¼–½ in.) deep and leave about 25–30 cm. (9–12 in.) between rows. Sow as thinly as possible by placing one seed every few inches, which will mean less thinning out when the seedlings have started to grow. Water regularly, especially in dry weather and keep free from weeds. Weeds will take nutrients from the soil and leave less for your plants to feed on.

Mustard takes only a couple of months from germination to harvesting, so it's possible to sow lines of seed every few weeks to have a constant supply. However, this does take up valuable space in the garden. Mustard is a good early crop to grow and once harvested, the space can be used for heat-loving crops in the summer months.

Use the leaves sparingly as the plants start to develop. Only take one or two from each plant at a time. Allow them to regrow before picking again.

Harvesting

To harvest the seed, the plants should be left until the last possible moment. Pods of seeds pop open when ripe and spray the seeds around, so to save missing it, place a cloth or piece of card around the plants in order to catch them. Otherwise pick pods and dry off for a day in the sun or in a bright airy spot. Pick the pods as the plant starts to lose its color and is dying back.

Container Growing

There doesn't appear to be any good reason why mustard plants can't be grown in containers, however, plants can grow to 90 cm. (3 ft.) tall so the pots or containers will need to be fairly large. Keep in a sunny spot, but don't keep indoors as mustard prefers a cooler temperature.

The pots should be well draining, but never allowed to dry out. Use fresh compost to get the most from your plants, although generally mustard seed will do well in most garden soils. Check on your seed packet for any other growing recommendations.

Using and storing mustard

Mustard seed will last for a year or more when kept in jars and stored out of direct light. After harvesting the pods, spread seeds out on a tray in a bright place for a few hours to dry before storing.

Mustard condiments can be made at home using simple recipes. Mustard poultices have been used for centuries—at one time mustard was known as the "singer's herb" because of its success in treating sore throats. Breathing in the vapor of boiling water poured over mustard seeds can help fight off colds and coughs.

Poppies

Although freshly baked poppy-seed bread is irresistible, poppies are, in fact, illegal to cultivate in some countries and regions. Check with the legislation locally before you sow poppy seeds in your garden.

When the flower has finished blooming, the opium poppy (*Papaver somniferum*) produces a latex in the seed pod that is commonly known as opium, and is processed into the drug heroin. The obvious dangers of heroin are the reason poppies aren't always legal to grow. However, the latex is also processed into a pure morphine and has been used as a medical pain-relieving drug for many years.

Over many parts of the world, poppies grow wild and are an attractive meadow flower, often found in packets of mixed wildflower or meadow seeds. Other varieties do not produce the same opiate as the opium poppy. They are an annual plant but will often reseed themselves in ideal conditions.

Growing advice

Seed should be sown *in situ* as poppies don't like to be replanted. Choose a sunny well-drained spot in the flower garden, or use as a border or edging plant. Dig over the ground and prepare by removing all perennial weeds and large stones; then rake or hoe the soil to a fine consistency. As with all seeds planted directly outside, they will have a better chance of germination if the soil is fine and well prepared beforehand.

Sow seed thinly as seedlings will need thinning out later on. Check your seed packet for regional variations in sowing times. Poppy seed can often be sown in spring or autumn, but regional and variety differences should be checked first.

Cover the seeds with soil and water gently. As long as the ground doesn't completely dry out, seed should germinate

fairly quickly. Never over-water. When seedlings are an inch high, they should be thinned to about 2.5 cm. (1 in.) apart. Keep weeds away to avoid nutrients being drawn from the soil. Weeds can also strangle the roots of young poppy plants.

When the plants have finished flowering, they produce a seed capsule that should be left as long as possible for the seeds inside to ripen. Gently tap the pod from time to time, and you will hear or feel the seeds rattling inside.

Leave the pods on the plant to reseed if they have had a successful

Container Growing

Poppies can be grown in containers, although they are originally a field crop so will probably do better in open ground. However, new hybrid varieties may be more suitable for container growing. Always make sure your containers or pots are well drained and do not allow them to completely dry out.

The "wild" or original varieties of poppy tend to grow to over 30 cm. (12 in.) high, so should be placed behind lower-growing plants to avoid overshadowing in a cramped space, such as a window box or other container.

year. However, if a very cold winter is expected or the flowers weren't as healthy as they could have been, collect the seed by removing pods when the seeds are ripe and try another location next year.

Plants that have been grown from hybrids will revert back to the original wild varieties—either *Papaver somniferous* (opium poppy) or *Papaver rhoeas* (corn or field poppy)—when left to reseed themselves. Hybrid varieties will need sowing every year to prevent this happening.

Using and storing poppy seed

Poppy seed can be collected and stored as soon as it is ripe and kept in labelled jars out of direct light. Poppy seed doesn't contain any opium or other adverse ingredients so whole seeds can be added safely to homemade breads, soups, curries, chutneys, and other recipes.

Seeds can be crushed and mixed with other ground spices. Poppy seed oil is processed for culinary use and also an artist's oil. The flowers of the red poppy are sometimes used to color wines and other products. However, all parts of the poppy, apart from the ripe seeds, are dangerous to consume.

Saffron

Saffron, at the time of writing, is probably the most expensive spice known to mankind. It takes around 150,000 flowers and hundreds of hours of labor to produce a couple of pounds of dried saffron threads. Only a small amount is used at a time so this is a good reason to grow it yourself. Saffron spice comes from the stigmas or fronds of the flower *Crocus sativus*, and is believed to originate in India. In recent years it has spread over many regions and is cultivated in Europe as well as Middle Eastern countries.

Saffron has been one of the most revered herbs for thousands of years and was cultivated for use as early as the eleventh century.

Growing advice

Although saffron is a hardy plant and will survive in many cooler climates, it may not flower in poor summers. A greenhouse or bright conservatory may be a better spot if you are in a region where summer sunshine is not very reliable. Plants are propagated from "corms," which resemble bulbs and in ideal conditions, will multiply every year. They can be left in the ground for three or four years, sometimes longer before they need to be dug up and separated.

Propagation by corms
Prepare a very sunny well-drained spot in the garden. Saffron likes rich soil so it's a good idea to dig in some well-rotted compost during the season before planting. Dig over the soil and remove any perennial weeds and large stones. Rake or hoe to a fairly fine consistency. Corms should be planted in mid-summer to flower the following year.

Container Growing

The saffron crocus will grow well in containers or large pots. Make sure they are well drained and filled with fairly rich fresh compost. In regions with shorter or unreliable summers, container growing may be the best way to achieve good results.

Position in the sunniest, warmest spot in the garden or in a conservatory or greenhouse. The flowers need a lot of sun to develop, so gently move containers around during the day to catch the sun if necessary.

Plant corms as you would in the garden, and allow enough space for each plant to grow. They may need repotting every year in fresh compost to keep the corms healthy and producing enough flowers.

Buy corms from a reliable supplier, and be sure to get the right variety—only *Crocus sativus* produces saffron. All other crocus varieties are inedible.

Sometimes larger corms planted earlier in the summer will flower in the same year as planting but generally, a year should be allowed before plants flower. Plant soon after buying as the corms will be healthier the fresher they are. Only a small amount of saffron will be available from each flower, so plant a whole line if possible. Dig a 10 cm. (4 in.) deep hole for each corm and allow about 10 cm. (4 in.) between them. Check on the growing recommendations on the packet for any variations in your region.

Let the soil dry out during the summer, but water from time to time in late summer or autumn when the flowers start appearing.

Leaves will grow taller than the flower stem and will stay green for many months after the plants have finished flowering. Leave them to die back naturally. If a very cold winter is expected, gently dig up the corms and plant in a container for the winter or keep them in a plastic bag with a little compost and store in a dark cool place in the house before planting out again when the weather warms up. They can also be protected with mulch or even a plastic cloche. A little attention goes a long way when growing your own saffron.

Harvesting

Whole flowers can be
collected just before opening
and stigmas removed
afterwards or, if the sun has
been kind and the flowers
are blooming, collect the
stigmas directly from
the flowers while
still on the plants.
This is quite fiddly and
will stain the fingertips
temporarily.

Using and storing saffron

Harvest saffron by pulling the stigmas
from the center of the flowers. Lay these saffron
threads on a tray carefully and dry very slowly in a cool oven, or in
the sun if possible, until completely dry. Store in an airtight jar out of
direct light.

Saffron has a distinctive honey/bitter taste and will color food as
well as flavoring it. Add to rice dishes such as paella and to many
savory and sweet recipes. Threads can be soaked in hot water for
a while to release the flavor or crumbled and added directly to
the cooking pot.

Further reading

Books

Grow Your Own, Ian Cooke (Skyhorse
   Publishing)
Your Backyard Herb Garden, Miranda Smith
   (Rodale)
Mini Farming, Brett Markham (Skyhorse
   Publishing)

Useful Websites
www.flower-and-garden-tips.com
www.botanical.com
www.linda-gray.co.uk

Index